Fort McIntosh: Its Times and Men

"Fort Pitt" and Its Times

"Logstown," on the Ohio

Three Historical Sketches

Second Book in the *Wilderness Wars in North America* Series

Fort McIntosh: Its Times and Men

"Fort Pitt" and Its Times

"Logstown," on the Ohio

Three Historical Sketches

by

Daniel Agnew, L.L.D.

Edited by
James A. Harris

esse quam videri

NW
est. 2002

NORMAL WARFARE PUBLICATIONS

Fort McIntosh: Its Times and Men
"Fort Pitt" and Its Times
"Logstown," on the Ohio
Three Historical Sketches

by
Daniel Agnew, L.L.D.

Edited by
James A. Harris

GRAPHICS AND COVER DESIGN BY

David A. Bock

PRODUCTION BY

Philip S. Bock

ISBN 0-9748690-2-3

Normal Warfare Publications
P. O. Box 35
Normal, IL 61761

www.normalwarfare.com

Originally published in 1893 and 1894.

This book is dedicated to our friend,

Bob Brynildson

of Falcon Heights, MN
for his unflinching support.

Table of Contents

Illustrations & Maps

Introduction

THE HONORABLE Daniel Agnew (1809–1902) was one of the earliest residents of Beaver, Pennsylvania. Born in Trenton, New Jersey, his family moved to Pennsylvania when he was still young. He graduated from Western University in Pittsburgh in 1825 and began to practice law. Agnew moved to Beaver in 1829. He became a member of the Whig Party and was appointed a judge in the 17th Judicial circuit in 1851. Agnew then served as Chief Justice of Pennsylvania from 1863–1878. After his retirement, he returned to Beaver, where he spent most of the remainder of life in the pursuit of local history.[1]

This edition reprints three short historical sketches Judge Agnew originally published in 1893 and 1894. The first, *Fort McIntosh: Its Times and Men,* provides a history of Fort McIntosh as well as information related to Fort Pitt during the later years of War of American Independence. The second essay, *"Fort Pitt" and Its Times,* covers aspects of the history of Fort Pitt not contained in the earlier work. The third work, *"Logstown" on the Ohio,* is a history of white relations with the Native American inhabitants of the village of Logstown, an important trading center during the 1740s and 1750s.

Judge Agnew was clearly a man of his times. His writing reflects the opinions and prejudices of most nineteenth century Americans. That is, he firmly believed in the inevitable progress of civilization over the wilderness. While he may have lamented the fate of the Native Americans, there can be little doubt that he believed that they must step aside for the sake of progress. Likewise, he did not doubt the righteousness of the colonial cause in the War of American Independence.

Agnew did not cite his sources, although it is clear that he relied heavily on such earlier works as Neville Craig's *In Olden Time*, and the Minutes of the Provincial Council. It is not within the scope of this edition to identify those sources. Judge Agnew's original foot-

Daniel Agnew

notes remain at the bottom of pages, marked with symbols. However he often fails to identify the people and places about which he writes. We have therefore edited these documents to provide the basic biographical and historical information that the modern reader would expect. They can be found as numbered endnotes at the end of each chapter. This work also contains an appendix of biographical remarks.

Many sources were used in obtaining the biographical information contained in the footnotes. Much of it was obtained through hours of surfing the internet. The number of genealogical pages consulted are too numerous to mention. As such, sources for basic biographical data such as the years of birth and death are not credited. However, internet addresses have been provided for those citations which contain original ideas and thoughts, or proved to be of unusual value. Of particular value were genealogy.com and rootsweb.com. For free on-line dictionaries, Virtuology.com is helpful. It contains James Grant Wilson and John Fiske, eds., *Appleton's Cyclopedia of American Biography,* Six volumes, New York: D. Appleton and Company, 1887–1889 & edited Stanley L. Klos, 1999. Also helpful is the Dictionary of Canadian Biography On-line at www.biographi. ca and the Biographical Directory of the United States Congress, at http://bioguide.congress.gov. Another helpful site is American National Biography On-line at http://anb.org, but it charges a fee.

Normal Warfare Publications is proud to present these three difficult to find historical sketches together in a single volume for the first time.

James A. Harris

Normal Warfare Publications

Notes:

[1] For biographical information on Judge Agnew see Joseph H. Bausman, *History of Beaver County Pennsylvania and Its Centennial Celebration,* 1:314–316.

Fort McIntosh

ITS TIMES AND MEN.

WITH

A HISTORICAL SKETCH

OF THE

FRENCH AND BRITISH CLAIMS IN THE NORTHWEST,
AND THEIR MEETING IN ARMS AT THE HEAD OF
THE OHIO, AND THE INDIAN INCURSIONS AND
OUTRAGES IN WESTERN PENNSYLVANIA
AND THE OHIO TERRITORY.

BY DANIEL AGNEW, LL. D.

Originally Published:

Pittsburgh
Myers, Skinkle & Co., Steam Printers, 523 Wood Street
1893.

Fort McIntosh:
Its Times and Men

THIS FORT WAS BUILT by General Lachlan McIntosh,[1] in the autumn of 1778, on the right bank of the Ohio river, and upon the high bluff where the town of Beaver now stands. It was a place marked by important events in the last century.

The circumstances which led to its construction cannot be fairly understood without a knowledge of the western territory as then existing. It was wild and uninhabited, except by hostile Indian tribes, controlled first by France, and then by Great Britain, Detroit being the center of influence of each in turn.

The events leading to its erection will be briefly sketched. France having entered the St. Lawrence at an early day, passed upward, settling Acadia, and founding Quebec, Montreal, and other towns on the river. Pursuing her way northwestward by the Ottawa river, she was first led to the discovery of the upper lakes, leaving Ontario and Erie to the left. As a consequence, her subjects and her missionaries entered on the territories bounding on Lakes George, Huron, Michigan and Superior. Making friends with the Indians, they spread over the northern country, reaching and partly crossing the Mississippi. Here these representatives of France, priest and chevalier, labored among them—for example, Mesnard, Le Carron, Allouez, Marquette, Joliet, La Salle, Hennepin, Frontenac, Champlain, and others, imprinting their names upon the soil on which they trod.[2]

From this "coign of vantage," then undisputed by any European power, they carried forward their conquests along the Illinois, Wabash and Ohio rivers; and borne onward upon the bosom of the "Father of Waters," finally came into touch with Spain in the south. Thus the interior of the continent was the first to be reached by Frenchmen, and the lillies of France planted there. In this spreading of the French dominion, the good will of the Indians was generally cultivated. In the beginning France was largely left in ignorance of Ontario and

Erie by her divergence up the Ottawa, and by the bold front of the warlike Iroquois, the Five Nations, afterwards known as the Six Nations, when joined by the Tuscaroras from the south. These warlike tribes occupied central and northern New York, extending westward and northward, and reaching to the St. Lawrence. They were known as the Mohawk, Oneidas, Onondagos, Cayugas and Senecas, finally joined by the Tuscaroras.

Afterwards descending Lakes Huron and St. Clair, and finding the straits leading into Lake Erie, France founded Detroit, which became the center of her western influence, and from which she controlled the Indian tribes, occupying what are now Ohio, Indiana, Illinois and Michigan.[3] It was not until nearly the middle of the 18th century she reached Presque Isle, (now Erie), and took possession of the surrounding region, reaching the Allegheny river, then called by them the Ohio. She planted forts at Presque Isle, Le Boueff, on upper French Creek, and Venango, at its mouth.[4]

France claimed the territory to the main Ohio, under an alleged discovery of the "La Belle Rivieur," by the Sieur La Salle, about sixty years before reaching Presque Isle, and was determined to hold possession even by force of arms.[5] In the year 1749, she sent an officer named Celeron down the Allegheny and Ohio, to plant there the evidence of her title.[6] This she did by burying along these streams leaden plates asserting her dominion. One of these plates, dated August 16, 1749, was dug up at the mouth of the Muskingum river, and another at Point Pleasant. A third was found at the mouth of French Creek, on the Allegheny, the "Ohio," as that river was called by them.

The following is a translation of the last, viz:

In the year 1749, reign of Louis XV, King of France, we Celeron, Commandant of a detachment by Monsieur, the Marquis of Gallisonier,[7] Commander in Chief of New France; to establish tranquility in certain Indian villages of these cantons, have buried this plate at the confluence of Loradakoin, this 29th of July, near the river Ohio, otherwise Beautiful River, as a monument of renewal of possession, which we have taken of the said river, and all its tributaries, and of all land on both sides, as far as the sources of said rivers; inasmuch as the preceding Kings of France have enjoyed this possession, and maintained it by their arms and by treaties, especially those of Ryswick, Utrecht, and Aix la Chapelle.

In the year 1753, Major Washington was sent by the Governor of Virginia to the forts on French Creek, to learn the purpose of the French in building them. In consequence of his information, early in the following year Virginia troops were sent to occupy the junction of the rivers at the head of the main Ohio, Virginia at that time claiming the surrounding territory.

The French Governor at Detroit,[8] learning from the visit of Washington and the attempt to hold the head of the Ohio, the intention of Great Britain to contest the claim of France, sent down the Allegheny a large force under Monsieur Coutrecouer, consisting of 300 canoes, 1,000 French and Indians, and 18 cannon, which dispersed the Virginia troops at the confluence of the Monongahela and Allegheny, and built Fort Du Quesne, named after the French Governor. Here France and England met in arms, and it now becomes necessary to take up the English side.[9]

As early as 1620, at Plymouth, in Massachusetts, and a few years earlier on the James river, in Virginia, the colonists from Great Britain began the settlements on the Atlantic coast, extending thence north and south. But the vast range of the Allegheny mountains, and the hostility of the Indians, long prevented the English from passing beyond this great mountain barrier into the western territory, their first ventures being south of the Ohio into the Kentucky region. It was nearly the middle of the 18th century that the designs of France becoming suspected, measures were taken to oppose her schemes and to prevent the Indian tribes occupying Western Pennsylvania, and the Ohio territory from taking part with France.

Conrad Weiser,[10] a citizen of Berks county, Pennsylvania, a surveyor familiar with some of the Indian tongues, was sent by the President and Council of Pennsylvania to learn the feelings of the tribes north of the Ohio. Setting out on the 11th of August, 1748, and crossing the Mountains he passed through the "Clearfields" (now Clearfield county,) thence to the Kiskiminetas, and crossing the Ohio, (the

Allegheny,) he came to the Beaver, visiting the Indian towns thereon; going thence to the main Ohio and up it to Logstown. He saw many Indians of different tribes, held councils with them, and learned their relations to the French.

In 1751, George Croghan sent out by Governor Hamilton,[11] of Pennsylvania, held councils and made treaties with the Indians at Logstown, learning much of their condition and designs.

The next, and probably the most important mission was that, before stated, of Washington to the French forts. Though then a young man, he was sent out by Governor Dinwiddie, of Virginia, in 1753.[12] At that time the common boundary between Pennsylvania and Virginia not being ascertained accurately, Virginia claimed all the territory at and surrounding the head of the Ohio. Washington reached Will's creek on the 14th of November, 1753, and there made his final preparation, passing the junction of the Monongahela and Allegheny and thence reaching Logstown on the right bank of the Ohio. From this point with three attendants he travelled northward to Venango, and thence to Fort Le Boueff, on French creek, where he delivered to the commandant his letter from Governor Dinwiddie. It was on his return from the French fort that our country had nearly lost the services of Washington, in the Revolution and in civil life. On the 28th of December, compelled to cross the Allegheny by a raft, made with difficulty with a single hatchet, by himself and Mr. Gist, his only companion,[13] Washington was thrown into the Allegheny in deep water by the force of the ice against his pole, and he and Mr. Gist barely escaped to Wainwright's island, (its modern name,) two miles above the junction of the rivers, where they passed the night. The channel on the eastern side which they crossed was open in the 20's, except where crossed by a mill dam, at which the writer has often fished in his boyhood. It is now closed I believe. Washington says, in his journal: "The cold was so intensely severe Mr. Gist had all his fingers and some of his toes frozen, and the water was shut up so hard that we found no difficulty in getting off the island on the ice in the morning."

It was now clear that France intended to hold the territory along the Ohio and at the junction of the rivers. This knowledge led

Robert Dinwiddie (1692–1770) was lieutenant governor of Virginia from 1751–1758. He took a leading roll in combating the French occupation of the Ohio Valley. Reproduced from R. A. Brock, ed., *The Official Records of Robert Dinwiddie*, Vol. II, Richmond, 1883.

25

George Washington at Age 25. Reproduced from Cyrus Townsend Brady, *Colonial Fights and Fighters,* New York, 1901.

Virginia, in April, 1754, to send out a small force under Col. Fry, to take possession of the junction and build a fort there. Lieut. Ward, with a few men was engaged in building the fort, when Contrecouer as before stated, reached the junction with the large force already mentioned. Ward surrendered, and the French engaged in building Fort Du Quesne, named after the French Governor at Detroit.[14]

Without entering into details, it may be said that Col. Fry having died, his Virginia command devolved on Major Washington, who after defeating a small force from Du Quesne, under Lieut. Jumonville, was in turn defeated by a larger force from the fort, compelled to surrender and to return to Virginia.[15]

The death of Jumonville was, however, the source of great French detraction of Washington. In the articles of capitulation his death was termed assassination, on which great stress has been laid by French historians. The charge evidently grew out of the French terms used, and the imperfect translation of Captain Vanbraam, a Dutchman. An officer of the regiment present at the surrender, wrote to a friend— "When Vanbraam returned with the French proposals we were obliged to take the sense of them from his mouth, it rained so hard that he could not give us a written translation of them, we could scarcely keep the candle lighted to read them by, and every officer there is ready to declare that there was no such word as assassination mentioned. The terms expressed were the death of Jumonville."[16]

Great Britain now determined to dislodge the French. For this purpose, after great preparations, she sent forward the expedition under General Braddock, with a portion of the flower of the British army. This unfortunate officer; on the 9th of July, 1755, was defeated with great slaughter near to the mouth of Turtle Creek, by the combined force of French and Indians from Fort Du Quesne, losing a large part of his army, himself mortally wounded and many of his finest officers killed.[17]

The next attempt to dislodge the French was made by an army under General John Forbes, in the year 1758. The army pursued a new route through Pennsylvania, by way of Bedford. An advance was sent forward in September, under the gallant Major Grant, who with his Highlanders, was defeated with terrible slaughter, on the hill near the fort since known as Grant's hill. General Forbes with the main army reached Du Quesne on the 25th of November, 1758, to find it abandoned by the French, and largely destroyed by fire.[18]

This was the last effort of the French to hold the head of the Ohio, but being in possession of Detroit and the Lakes their baleful influence over the Indians continued. In 1760, after the fall of Quebec and Niagara, the English army under General Amherst, still advancing, the French governor surrendered Detroit and Mackinaw.[19] The treaty of Paris, in 1763, followed, by which France ceded to Great Britain her pretention to Nova Scotia or Acadia, and Canada, and all her claims east of the Mississippi river, except the Isle of Orleans.

But the Indians continued hostile, and Pontiac the head of the Ottawas, and probably the greatest Indian chief of the last century, in the year 1762 founded his great confederacy of the western tribes, terminating in a general council at Ecores in April, 1763.[20] His purpose was the extermination of the whites and the overthrow of the English power in the west. He waged war against the British for more than a year with great violence. As a consequence the entire western territory was unsafe to the whites. The Indians laid siege to Fort Pitt, which succeeded Fort Du Quesne. It was to relieve this fort that Col. Henry Boquet and a force of about 500 men were sent by the Pennsylvania route. In August, 1763, the Indians discovering his approach, ambushed his force at Bushy Run, in Westmoreland county, but after a most sanguinary battle were defeated and Fort Pitt relieved. From thence in the autumn of 1764, Col. Boquet made his expedition against the Indians in the territory, now of the State of Ohio.[21]

As his route passed directly over the Beaver plain, where Fort McIntosh was afterwards built and his journal minutely describes the country approaching and near to the fort a portion of it may be inserted here, viz:

Things being thus settled the army decamped from Fort Pitt on Wednesday October 3, and marched about one mile and a half, over a rich level country with stately timber, to camp No. 2, a strong piece of ground pleasantly situated with plenty of water and food for cattle.*

Thursday, October 4, having proceeded about two miles, came to the Ohio at the beginning of the narrows, and from thence followed the course of the river, along flat gravelly beach, about six miles and a quarter, with two islands on the left, the lowermost about six miles long, with a rising ground running across and gently sloping on both sides to its banks, which are high and upright.

---

* (REMARK.—Camp No. 2, must have been about a half or three quarters of a mile below the old Penitentiary site.)

At the lower end of this island, the army left the river, marching through good land, broken with small hollows to camp No. 3, this day's march being nine miles and a quarter.[*]

Friday, October 5, in this day's march the army passed through Logstown, situated 17 miles, one half and 57 perches from Fort Pitt. This place was noted before the last war for the trade carried on there by the English and French, but its inhabitants, the Sha-wanese and Delawares abandoned it in the year 1750. The lower town extended about sixty perches over a bottom to the foot of a low steep ridge, on the summit of which stood the upper town commanding a most agreeable prospect over the lower and quite across the Ohio, which is about 500 yards wide here, and by its majestic current adds much to the beauty of the place. Proceeding beyond Logstown through a fine country, interspersed with hills, rich valleys, watered by many rivulets and covered with stately timber, came to camp No. 4, on a level piece of ground, with a thicket in the rear, a small precipice round the front with a run of water at the foot, and good food for cattle. This days march was nine miles one-half and fifty-three perches.[**]

Saturday, October 6, at about three miles distance came again to the Ohio, pursuing its course half a mile farther, and then turn-ing off over a steep ridge crossed the Big Beaver Creek, which is twenty perches wide, the ford stony and pretty deep. It runs through a rich vale, with a pretty strong current, its banks high, the upland adjoining it very good, the timber tall and young.[***]

About a mile below its confluence with the Ohio stood formerly a large town on the steep bank, built by the French of square

---

[*] (REMARKS.—The route described as by the narrows and the islands on the left (Davis' and Nevilles,) and the departure at the foot of Nevilles prove conclusively that the march was on the right bank of the Ohio.)

[**] (REMARKS.—This account conclusively establishes Logstown as on the north side of the Ohio, a fact confirmed by Hutchin's map, and the journals of Conrad Weiser (1748,) and Frederick Post (1758.) Post's second journal (1758,) states that the Indians had a large cornfield on the south side. This explains how a late impression has prevailed that Logstown was on the south side.)

[***] (REMARKS.—The crossing was evidently just below where the Beaver toll bridge stands.)

Colonel Henry Bouquet (1719–1765) was a Swiss officer serving in the 60th Regiment. He defeated the Ohio tribes at the Battle of Bushy Run and commanded the British expedition into the Ohio Country in 1764.

logs, with stone chimneys, for some of the Shawanese, Delawares and Mingoes, who abandoned it in the year 1758, when the French abandoned Fort Du Quesne.*

Near the fording of Beaver creek also stood about seven houses which were deserted and destroyed by the Indians after their defeat on Bushy Run, when they forsook all the remaining settlements in this part of the country as has been mentioned above.**

Camp No. 5, the journal of Boquet states, was seven miles one-fourth and 57 perches from the Big Beaver, the whole distance marched on the 6th of October being about twelve miles.

On the 8th of October the army crossed the Little Beaver creek.

At this time (1764) the Big Beaver entered into the Ohio by two channels which were there in 1829 when the writer saw it.

The western, or smaller channel, an ordinary high water outlet, was separated from the main channel by a large island, containing a few perches over twelve acres, which in 1792 Was surveyed by Daniel Leet into two outlets.[22]

This island was largely carried away, by the great flood of the 10th of February, 1832. Subsequent floods carried all away leaving it a stony bed, as it now appears, its fate being similar to that of Killbuck (or Smoky Island) at the mouth of the Allegheny river, which when the writer knew it contained about seven or eight acres and was cultivated.

The relief of Detroit by the British, and their possession of the lake region, put an end to Pontiac's war. The Indian troubles in the west, however, did not cease, but culminated in 1774, in the war known as Lord Dunmore's.[23] This scarcely had ended when a new cause fanned the embers of Indian hostility—the war of the Revolution.

─────────────

* (REMARK.—This town stood about a half or two-thirds of a mile below Market street in Beaver on the property of the late David Minis.)

** (REMARKS.—This hamlet was known as Sawkunk or Sawkung, and must have stood on the island at the mouth of the creek, or on the "Stone" property west side of the Big Beaver, as Frederick Post in his second journal (1758,) says, that on leaving Sawkunk he crossed the Big Beaver going up to Fort Du Quesne.)

England, regardless of the ties of blood and the dictates of humanity, by every influence within her power, persuaded the savages to lift the tomahawk and sharpen the scalping knife against the colonists. Outrage and barbarity followed the Indian footsteps across the Ohio river, and even to and beyond the Allegheny mountains. The entire west became unsafe for white settlement.

It was during this period it became necessary to check their savage inroads, by forming a military department for the west, with headquarters at Fort Pitt. From September, 1775, until 1777, Fort Pitt had been occupied only by Virginia militia, about one hundred, under Capt. John Neville.[24] On the first day of June, 1777, Brigadier General Edward Hand,[25] of the continental army, under the orders of Washington, reached Fort Pitt to form the military department for the west. Hand projected several expeditions against the Indians, both north and west, but the difficulties of enlisting and maintaining troops in this quarter compelled their abandonment. It was Washington's design to reduce Detroit from this quarter, but the war on the Atlantic coast and the difficulty in the west, prevented its accomplishment. General Hand was an able officer, and did all in his power to carry the war into the Indian strongholds, but was met by obstacles on every hand. These were greatly increased by the desertion to the enemy of Alexander McKee, Matthew Elliott and the two Girtys, Simon and James; followed afterward by George Girty.[26]

These men became implacable enemies of the colonists, making their headquarters at Detroit, thence visiting the Ohio territory, inciting the Indians against the whites; the Girtys even accompanying their incursions into the settlements across the Ohio river, and participating in their barbarities. These were made more brutally cruel by the inhuman order of Lieutenant-Governor Henry Hamilton, the British commandant at Detroit, "who ordered the payment of a bounty for scalps, but none for prisoners. As a consequence, few prisoners were brought to Detroit, when scalps alone commanded a premium.[27]

In this state of affairs General Hand was recalled, at his own request, in the spring of 1778, and Washington appointed Brigadier General Lachlan McIntosh as his successor in the command at Fort Pitt. He was a Georgian, and an officer of great merit, esteemed by

Washington, who regretted his departure from the east, and said of him:

> His firm disposition and equal justice, his assiduity and good understanding, added to his being a stranger to all parties in that quarter, pointed him out as a proper person."

Lachlan McIntosh was a son of John More McIntosh, chief of a branch of the Clan McIntosh, in Scotland, who with one hundred of his highland clansmen accompanied Governor James Oglethorpe to Georgia, in 1736, and settled in what is now McIntosh county. Lachlan was born on the 17th day of March, 1725, near Inverness; in Scotland. His early years were spent in various pursuits. While a clerk in Charleston, S. C., he was called, September 16, 1776, to the command of the first Georgia regiment, and subsequently was made Brigadier General of three regiments. He soon accepted a command in the central army, under Washington, and while in this position was sent, in 1778, to Fort Pitt. He reached Fort Pitt in August, 1778.

The narrative thus discovers the embarrassments which General McIntosh encountered in taking command of the western department. Neither men nor the munitions of war could be easily had, and he was encompassed by hostile tribes, whose movements in a wild and uninhabited country, could not be foreseen or met. The redmen were led on also by whites even more savage, traitors to kin and country, and familiar with the affairs of the colonists. The savages lay in wait at every turn, coming when least expected, killing and scalping men, women and children.

Washington's designs on Detroit from Fort Pitt being prevented by the condition of affairs on the Atlantic and in the west, his instructions to McIntosh embraced only expeditions against the western Indians. McIntosh also had Detroit in view, but was without orders or means. The season being late, provisions scarce, and enlistments tardy, he was retarded in his movements, and concluded to prepare for future operations. This he did by erecting a fort nearer to the point from which he could march either westward into Ohio, or northward to Detroit. His own account is found in his letter to Vice-President Bryan,[28] dated Fort Pitt, December 29th, 1778. He says:

General Lachlan McIntosh (1725–1806) was commander of American forces on the Ohio from May, 1778 until May 1779. He ordered the construction of Fort McIntosh. Reproduced from Louise Phelps Kellogg, *Frontier Advance on the Ohio,* Madison, 1916.

That notwithstanding the season was so late that we could not get sufficiency of supplies, and the men so tedious before they came and joined me, with many other difficulties I had to encounter, I erected a good, strong fort for the reception and security of pris-oners and stores upon the Indian side of the Ohio, below Beaver Creek, with barracks for a regiment; and another upon Muskingum river, where Col. Boquet had one formerly; near Tuscarawas, about one hundred miles from this place, which I expect will keep the

Henry Laurens (1724–1792) of South Carolina was president of the Continental Congress from November 1777 to December 1778. Fort Laurens, at present-day Coshocton, OH, was named in his honor. Reproduced from Louise Phelps Kellogg, Frontier Advance on the Ohio, Madison, 1916.

> savages in awe, and secure the peace of the frontiers effectually in this quarter hereafter, if they are well supplied; and will also facilitate any further enterprises that may be attempted that way.

The fort on the Tuscarawas was named "Laurens," after Henry Laurens, President of Congress.[29]

This letter proves that Fort McIntosh was of much greater importance than Col. Brodhead was disposed to accord to it. Indeed

35

from his letter, it is evident, that Brodhead, who was subordinate to McIntosh, was animated by a personal feeling, which sometimes arises in the army. His personal difficulty with Col. Gibson, and retirement from command of Fort Pitt, possibly indicate a want of good temper.[30] In his letter to General Armstrong[31] dated at Fort Pitt, April 16, 1779, he said:

> And it was owing to the General's (McIntosh's) determination to take Detroit, the very romantic building called Fort McIntosh, was built by the hands of hundreds who would rather have fought than wrought."

In Brodhead's letter to General Greene,[32] August 2, 1779, he writes:

> General McIntosh, was not regardless of the stores, in some respects, in others he was. The hobbyhorse he built at Beaver creek, occasioned a delay of military operations and consequently an useless consumption of stores, &c.

But Brodhead, who succeeded General McIntosh in the command, found by two years and a half experience, it was harder to conduct military operations in a wilderness, and where men and munitions were difficult to be had, than his condemnation of McIntosh warranted.

In order to make Fort McIntosh more easy of communication and supply, General McIntosh cut a road from Fort Pitt to Fort McIntosh. This was essential to his plan of supplying the latter for future operations, and must have been opened on the south side of the Ohio. The old route by which Col. Boquet marched in 1764, was utterly unsafe to supply trains. Such wagon trains would have been constantly exposed to the attacks of the savages, who were always found on the north side and alert on the lookout. While it is not stated where the road was opened, it is quite certain it was the same that comes down to the Ohio through the gap directly opposite the fort. This road was used by Brodhead when he came into command, and has since been known as the "Brodhead road."

Fort McIntosh is described by Arthur Lee,[33] one of the commissioners of the United States, to treat with the western Indians, who reached the fort, in December, 1784, the treaty being concluded there in January, 1785.

This description is contained in his journal, and as parts are not only interesting, but directly connected with the fort, they may be introduced here. He says:

> On the 17th of December 1784, we embarked on the Monongahela and soon entered the Ohio on our way to Fort McIntosh.

After describing Montours Island, (Neville's) and Logstown, he proceeds:

> From Logstown to the mouth of Beaver creek is — miles and from thence to Fort McIntosh one mile. This fort is built of well hewed logs with four bastions, its figure is an irregular square, the face to the river being longer than the side to the land. It is about equal to a square of fifty yards, is well built and strong against musketry; but the opposite side of the river commands it entirely, and a single piece of artillery from thence would reduce it.*

He continues:

> This fort was built by us during the war, and is therefor not noted on Hutchin's map. The place was formerly a large Indian settlement, and French trading place. There are peach trees still remaining. It is a beautiful plain extending about two miles along the river and one back to the hills, surrounded on the east by Beaver creek; and on the west by a small run, (Two Mile) which meanders through a most excellent piece of meadow ground full of shell bark hickory, black walnut and oak. About one mile and a half up

---

* (REMARKS—This is true, but it must be remembered, that there was no enemy to approach the fort on that side. It was subject to attack only from the same side with itself and there it was strong against musketry.)

the Beaver creek, there enters a small but perennial stream (Brady run) very fit for a mill seat.

On the 28th of December he says:

> Some of the officers getting merry late at night, ordered the artillery company to draw out the cannon and fire them in the midst of the garrison. One of them was accordingly fired. The commanding officer immediately ordered the whole garrison under arms, and the artillery officer to countermand the firing; he refused, upon which the other ordered him under arrest. The next officer in command of the artillery walking aside told the men to do as they thought proper; they hesitated to obey the commanding officer, and he ran his sword through one of them. This soon produced a withdrawal of the artillery. In the meantime the troops were all under arms, and drunken officers at the head of companies were giving contrary orders, swearing at and confounding the men. Upon this General Butler and myself sent for Major T——, the commanding officer, Col. Harmar being at Fort Pitt, and directed him to order the garrison immediately to their quarters; which being done the tumult subsided.[34]

Others speak of the fort as a regular stockade work, defended by six pieces of cannon and having a covered way to the river for water. The southwest bastion stood within twenty or twenty-five feet of the termination of the present Market street, in Beaver.

In the autumn of 1778, the Indians were very troublesome. They besieged Fort Laurens and kept it in constant alarm. The troops there under the command of Col. Gibson, were reduced to great straits, living on herbs and boiled hides, and were relieved, by General McIntosh, when suffering starvation.

A letter from Genl. McIntosh to Col. Lochry,[35] Lieut. of Westmoreland county dated January 29, 1779, says:

> I am informed that Capt. Clark, of the eighth Pennsylvania Regiment,[36] who was sent to command an escort to Fort Laurens, as he was returning with a sergeant and fourteen men, three miles this side of that fort, was attacked by Simon Girty, and a party of

Mingoes, who killed two of our men and wounded four and took one prisoner. I am also informed that a large party of the same people are set off to strike the inhabitants about Ligonier and Blackleg creek, and send you this express to inform you of it, that you may acquaint the neighborhood and be on your guard.

As a consequence of hardships, disappointments and vexatious delays, the spring of 1779, found Gen'l. McIntosh sick, and weary of his command, and he was recalled at his own request. He returned to Philadelphia, in April, 1779.

Daniel Brodhead, Colonel of the 8th Pennsylvania Regiment succeeded him. His letters portray the difficulties and dangers attending his command. In a postscript to a letter to General Washington, dated at Fort Pitt, July 31, 1779, he writes:

I have just learned that two soldiers have lately been killed at Fort Laurens, two boys on Wheeling Creek, two boys taken on Raccoon Creek, and one man slightly wounded, and a soldier last evening killed at Fort McIntosh, and a soldier slightly wounded. The inhabitants are so intent on going to Kentuck and the Falls of the Ohio, I fear I shall have few volunteers.

September 23d, 1779, writing from Pittsburgh to President Reed,[37] the Colonel says:

My officers and soldiers are exceedingly ragged, the soldiers naked, and I am unfortunately greatly distressed for want of clothing and money to relieve their necessities. Insomuch that unless more regard is paid to the aid of the troops, I must shortly request his Excellency, the Commander-in-Chief, to appoint another person to take the command, and give me leave to hand him my commission.

Also,

If our State or its Legislature have not yet allowed a greater bounty for recruits, I fear most of my good men whose terms are expired, will enter the Virginia corps.

Colonel Daniel Brodhead (1736–1809) of the 8th Pennsylvania Regiment arrived at Fort Pitt as second-in-command in March, 1778. He served as commander from April, 1779 until 1781. Reproduced from Louise Phelps Kellogg, *Frontier Retreat on the Upper Ohio,* Madison, 1917.

In another letter from Pittsburgh to President Reed, April 27, 1780, referring to four companies to be raised for the defence of the frontier, he says:

> I hope these companies when raised will be ordered to this district where the enemy are remarkably hostile. Between forty and fifty men, women and children have been killed and taken from what are now called the counties of Yoghagania, Monongalia and Ohio, since the first of March, but no damage has been done in the county of Westmoreland.

These counties embraced Fayette, Greene, Washington and Allegheny, and were so named by Virginia when she claimed this region, and attempted to govern it through Dr. Connolly and his lieutenants.[38]

In numerous letters Colonel Brodhead made similar complaints of the destitution of his troops. The Secretary of War, writing to President Reed, July 31, 1780, said:

> Colonel Brodhead's apprehensions of being reduced to the necessity of using force to obtain provisions, seem to be too justly founded.

Writing to President Reed September 16, 1780, Colonel Brodhead said: "The whole garrison went out led by Sergeants, who being asked the cause answered, that the troops had been five days without bread." On a promise of relief, they withdrew to quarters.

But the necessity soon came, and in his order, September 21, 1780, Brodhead instructed Capt. Sam Brady[39] to use compulsion to obtain food rather than that the troops should suffer. The condition of the troops in the Western Department, including Fort McIntosh, was evidently most deplorable.

In reference to the Indians, Colonel Brodhead, writing to General Washington, March 8, 1780, said:

> The savages have already begun their hostilities; last Sunday they killed five men at a sugar camp on Raccoon Creek, and took prisoners three boys and three girls.

Again, May 11th, 1780, he wrote to Major Slaughter:[40]

> The county of Westmoreland is again infested with the cursed Mingoes. The inhabitants are flying from every quarter, and it will be necessary for you to keep a look out where you are. I have not a sufficient party that can, at any rate, be spared from the garrison either to pursue or waylay the villains, and I shall be much obliged to you for sending fifteen or twenty of your best men to enable me to send out a sufficient party for a few days.

In a letter to Timothy Pickering,[41] July 21, 1780, he gives an account of an attack upon a body of Indians who had crossed the Ohio, a short distance above the present town of Industry. He said:

> A few days ago I received intelligence of a party of thirty odd Wyandot Indians having crossed the Ohio five miles below Fort McIntosh, and that they had hid their canoes upon the shore. I immediately ordered out two parties of the nearest militia to go in search of them, and cover the harvesters. At the same time Capt. McIntyre[42] was detailed with a party to form an ambuscade opposite the enemies' craft. Five men who were reaping in a field discovered the Indians; and presuming their number was small, went out to attack them, but four of them were immediately killed, and the other taken prisoner, before the militia were collected. But they were attacked by Capt. McIntyre's party on the river, and many of them were killed and wounded, two canoes were sunk, and the prisoner retaken, but the water was so deep our men could not find the bodies of the savages, and therefore the number killed can not be ascertained. The Indians left in their craft two guns, six blankets, eleven tomahawks, eleven paint bags, eight ear wheels, a large brass kettle, and many other articles. The Indians informed the prisoner that fifteen Wyandots were detached to Hanna's town; upon receiving this information, another party was immediately detached up the Allegheny river with two Delaware Indians to take the tracks, and make pursuit, but as the party has not yet returned, I cannot inform you of its success.

In a subsequent letter of September 17, 1780, to Col. David Shepherd,[43] he says:

Fort McIntosh, at the mouth of Big Beaver Creek, present-day Beaver, Pennsylvania. A 19th-Century engraving from George Dallas Alberts, *Frontier Forts of Western Pennsylvania*, volume II, 1916.

CAPTAIN SAMUEL BRADY.

Captain Samuel Brady (1756–1795) of the 8th Pennsylvania Regiment. Engraving by Richardson reproduced from Col. Frank Triplett, *Conquering the Wilderness,* Chicago, 1883.

> They, (the messengers,) likewise inform me, that in the attack made by Capt. McIntyre's party on the Wyandot warriors, eighteen or nineteen were killed, and some are still missing.

The party of Indians ambuscaded by Capt. McIntyre, must have crossed at "Safe Harbor," nearly opposite the present town of Industry. There is there on the south side a long stretch of deep water.

Throughout 1780 and 1781; the Indians continued hostile.

Writing from Fort Pitt to General Washington, Aug. 23d, 1781, Col. Brodhead said an expedition against Sandusky was in contemplation, and the troops would rendezvous at Fort McIntosh, on the 4th and 5th days of September. Next day he wrote to Capt. John Clark, commanding Fort McIntosh:

> I have this moment received certain intelligence, that the enemy are coming against us in great force, and that particularly against your post. You will immediately put your garrison in the best posture of defence, and lay in as large quantities of water as you can, clear the bank from about you, and receive them coolly. They intend to decoy your garrison, but you will guard against their stratagem, and defend the fort to the last extremity.

It does not appear, however, that the attack was made.

In the summer of 1781, quite a breeze sprang up at Fort Pitt between Col. Brodhead and a large number of officers in his command, headed by Col. John Gibson. They disputed his authority as the chief commander of the fort. Charges were made against him, and a court martial asked for.

In his letter to General Washington, dated at Fort Pitt, September 6, 1781, he says:

> Col. Gibson still continues to counteract me, and the officers who favor his claim refuse my orders, others refuse his, and things are in the utmost confusion.

He adds, in a postscript:

> I have arrested Col. Gibson on August 30th, for assuming the chief command at this fort, contrary to the articles and discipline of war, thereby inciting and encouraging meetings and sedition amongst a number of officers of this department.

On or about the same date, September 6th, 1781, Brodhead resigned the command, and soon afterwards Col. John Gibson was assigned to the department by Gen'l Washington. Brodhead, however, was a good officer and merited a better fate than that which befell him at Fort

Pitt. The real causes which led to his differences with Col. Gibson and a portion of his officers may not be fully developed at this late day, and probably need not be. He successfully conducted several expeditions against the Indians both north and west, but the inadequacy of means at Fort Pitt limited them to a small scale.

Col. Gibson was soon superseded by Brigadier General Wm. Irvine,[44] an officer of merit, who continued in command until after the close of the Revolutionary War. A few extracts from his letter to Gen'l Washington, dated at Fort Pitt, December, 1781, will give some idea of the state of affairs there and in the west. He says:

> I never saw troops cut so truly deplorable a figure. Indeed when I arrived no man would believe from their appearance that they were soldiers—and it would be difficult to determine whether they were white men, and though they do not yet come up to my wishes, they are some better.

He also refers to the enormous consumption of public stores, and says the magazine was nearly exhausted.

He gives an account of the failure of Gen'l Geo. Rogers Clark's expedition against the western Indians from the Falls of the Ohio.[45]

Capt. Craig, (Major Isaac), was forty days in returning from the Falls with a remnant of the artillery, throwing away the carriages on account of the low water. Clark was unable to prosecute his expedition for want of men, and his provisions were largely spoiled. Great fear arose of a force from Detroit.[46]

Col. Loughrey, (Lieut. of Westmoreland County,) on his way to join Clark with 100 men and a small detachment left by Clark at the mouth of the Miami to meet Loughrey, were waylaid by the Indians and British and all killed and taken, not a man escaping.

In this letter Gen'l Irvine suggested the abandonment of Fort Pitt, except a block house on the north bastion, and the building of a fort at the mouth of Chartier's creek to supersede Fort Pitt and Fort McIntosh. He was fearful the enemy from Detroit might surprise the latter, and make it the means of laying the country waste.

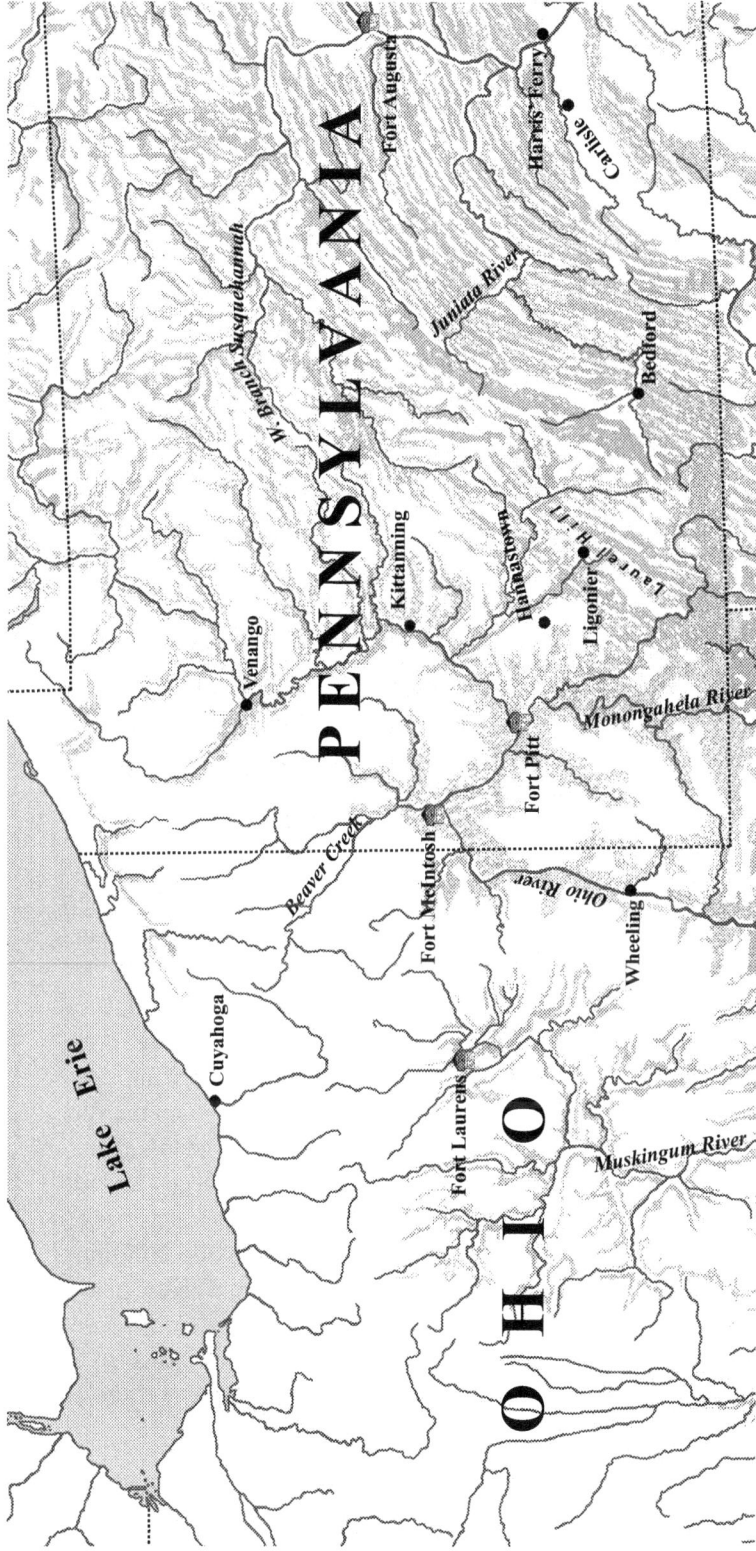

Western Pennsylvania and Eastern Ohio during the War of American Independence, 1775–1783.

No fort was built at Chartier's, and the enemy never came from Detroit, yet the letter gives a gloomy and no doubt a truthful account of the affairs in the western department at that time.

As the Indians were gradually pressed westward; the occupation of Fort McIntosh became less important, and in 1783, was suffered to go out of repair, besides suffering from the lawless trespasses of the settlers passing down the Ohio on their way to Kentucky. Brigadier General William Irvine was still in command at Fort Pitt. The troops having left, it was intended to let the fort go into the possession of the State of Pennsylvania, the State then having a reservation of 3,000 acres at the mouth of the Big Beaver. Accordingly the following instructions were given by Gen'l Irvine on the 23rd of September, 1783.

Instructions for Wm. Lee, Sergeant, and John McClure:

You are to take immediate charge of the fort buildings and public property now remaining at Fort McIntosh, for and in behalf of the State of Pennsylvania, (except two pieces of iron cannon, and some water casks, the property of the United States,) and three thousand acres of land reserved for the use of the State: when the tract is surveyed you will attend and make yourselves acquainted with the lines; in the meantime you will consider it extending two miles up and down the river, and two miles back; you will take care that no waste is committed, or timber cut down or carried off the premises, and prohibit buildings to be made or any persons making settlements or to reside thereon, or from even hunting encampments; nor are any more families to be permitted than your own to live in the barracks, or on any part of the tract. In case of necessity for reoccupying the post for the United States, you are to give up the fort to the orders of the commanding Continental officer at this place, retaining only such part of the building as may be necessary for you to live in. But if the troops should be so numerous as not to afford room for you, you will, in that case, occupy the buildings without the works, or build for yourselves in some convenient place, but you will on no account whatever quit the place without orders from the Executive Council of Pennsylvania, or their agents, so to do, whose directions you will thereafter obey in all matters relative to said post, and tract of land. In case of lawless violence or persons attempting to settle by force, or presuming to destroy anything on the I premises, you will apply to Michael Hoofnagle, Esq., or some other Justice of the Peace, for Westmoreland county. For your care and trouble in performing in the several matters herein required, you may put in grain and labor any quantity of ground not exceeding one hundred acres, and keep and raise stock to the number of fifty head of horned cattle and eight horses. You will govern yourselves by these instructions, until the pleasure of the Honorable Council is signified to you, and you will give up peaceable possession to them or their order, whenever they think proper.

Given under my hand at Fort Pitt, September 23rd, 1783.

WM. IRVINE, B. Gen'l.

We severally engage to conform to the foregoing instructions to us by Gen'l Irvine.

Witness: H. LEE,
    JOHN ROSE   JOHN MCCLURE.[47]

The 3,000 acres of reserved land referred to form an interesting history connected with the fort and will be explained hereafter.

John Rose, the witness to this paper, known as Major Rose, was an interesting character. His real name was Henri Gustav Rosenthal, a Russian nobleman. Involved in a duel, he killed his antagonist and fled his country, coming to America. He was a fine looking young gentleman, spoke the French language, and having studied surgery; became surgeon of the 7th Pennsylvania Regiment. Owing to jealousies he resigned and went into the navy, was taken prisoner, exchanged, returned to Pennsylvania, reentered the line and finally became aid to General Irvine at Fort Pitt, performed duty there, and in the fall of 1783 became secretary of the Council of Censors of Pennsylvania.

During all this time he kept his secret. In 1784, having received immunity from his sovereign, he sailed for Europe; before sailing having revealed his secret to General Irvine.

Fort McIntosh was fated to remain not long unoccupied by the United States troops. In 1784 the government concluding to treat with the western Indians it became necessary to reoccupy the fort. The treaty was contemplated at first to be held at Cuyahoga (now Cleveland) but was changed to Fort McIntosh. This can be told in the words of Col. Josiah Harmar's letter to President Dickinson,[48] viz:

> *Camp near Fort Pitt on the Indian shore, the*
> *western side of the Allegheny river, December 5, 1784.*

Sir:—I have the honor to inform your Excellency and the Hon. Council, of the arrival of the first detachment of Pennsylvania troops, composed of Captain Douglass' company of artillery and Captain Finney's company of infantry at this place on the 18th of October last.

The second detachment, composed of Captain Zeigler and Captain McCurdy's companies of infantry arrived here on the 29th, of the same month.[49]

We have remained in this position 'till to-day, in hourly expectation of the commissioners, they have just arrived, and upon consultation, considering the advanced season of the year, the difficulties of supplies, expense of transportation, etc., to Cuyahoga, they have resolved to hold the treaty at Fort McIntosh, thirty miles distant from Fort Pitt down the Ohio river.

In Consequence of their resolve, the troops marched this morning from their encampment for Fort McIntosh, the tents, baggage, etc., are to go by water. Mr. Alexander Lowry, messenger to the commissioners, was dispatched this day to Cuyahoga with an invitation to the Indians to assemble at Fort McIntosh.[50]

The fort is in very bad order and will require considerable repairs before the troops can have comfortable winter quarters.

The commissioners on part of the United States were George Rogers Clark, Richard Butler and Arthur Lee. Those on part of Pennsylvania were Col. Samuel I. Atlee and Col. Francis Johnston.[51]

The treaty consummated by the United States is not important to the present subject, excepting its first article, which provided for the surrender by the Indians, of all prisoners "white and black" held by them. Many of the prisoners were delivered at Fort McIntosh in

1785, and among them, an early and most respected citizen of Beaver, the late James Lyon, Esq. He had been captured when quite a child, in the year 1782, near to Turtle Creek, Westmoreland county, upon his father's farm, through which the Pittsburgh and Greensburg turnpike afterwards ran.

The treaty by the State is thus referred to by Col. Harmar in a letter to President Dickenson, dated at Fort McIntosh, February 8, 1785.

> The honorable the State commissioners Col. Atlee and Col. Johnston, by this time I imagine must have arrived at Philadelphia, by whom your excellency and the honorable council will hear of the satisfactory conclusion of the treaty with the Indians at this post.
>
> This garrison is at length by hard fatigue of the troops, put into tolerable order. I beg to observe to your excellency and the honorable council that unless some person is directed to remain here, that immediately upon my marching from hence, it will be demolished by the emigrants to Kentucky.
>
> Previous to our arrival here they had destroyed the gates, drawn all the nails from the roofs, taken off all the boards, and plundered it of every article. I would therefore recommend (for the benefit of the State) to your Excellency and Honorable Council to adopt some mode for its preservation, otherwise immediately upon leaving it, it will again go to ruin.

A confirmation of this opinion is found in a paragraph of the old Pittsburgh Gazette of June 2, 1787, entitled "Growth of travel" lately republished, viz:

> Since the tenth of October, 1786 to May 12th, 1787, there has passed down the Ohio river for Kentucky 177 boats, 2,689 people, 1,333 horses, 766 cattle, 102 wagons and one phaeton. The account was taken from a journal kept by the adjutant at Fort Harmar[52] at Muskingum. A number passed in the night unobserved.

The intention to remove from the fort soon led to a petition of David Duncan and John Finley, Indian traders, dated February 26, 1785, to the President and Council to take charge of the fort, with license to trade with the Indians.[53]

But the troops continued to occupy and Col. Harmar, on the 24th of May, 1785 reported the following officers at the fort, viz:

JOSIAH HARMAR, *Lieutenant. Colonel.*
WALTER FINNEY, *Captain.*[54]
DAVID ZEIGLER, *Captain.*
WM. MCCURDY, *Captain.*
THOMAS DOUGLASS, *Captain.*[55]
JOSEPH ASHTON, *Lieutenant.*[56]
STEWART HERBERT, *Lieutenant.*[57]
ESCURIUS BEATTY, *Lieutenant.*[58]
THOMAS DOYLE, *Lieutenant.*[59]
JOHN ARMSTRONG, *Ensign.*[60]
EBENEZER DENNY, *Ensign.*[61]
NATHAN MCDOWELL, *Ensign.*[62]
JOHN MCDOWELL, *Surgeon.*[63]
RICHARD ALLISON, *Mate.*[64]

On the 1st of June, 1785, Col. Harmar reported at present fit for duty in the infantry 156 men, present sick five; of the artillery present fit for duty forty, present sick two.

The lovers of sport will be interested in the following letter of Col. Harmar, dated Fort McIntosh, June 21st, 1785, to Col. Francis Johnston.

I wish you were here to view the beauties of Fort McIntosh. What think you of pike of 25 pounds, perch 15 to 20 pounds, catfish 40 pounds, bass, pickerel, sturgeon, &c. You certainly would enjoy yourself. It is very fortunate there is such an abundance of fish, as the contractor for this place sometime past has failed in his supplies of beef.

This would be a glorious season for Col. Wood,[65] or any extravagant lover of strawberries, the earth is most abundantly covered with then; we have them in such plenty, that I am almost surfeited with them; the addition of fine rich cream is not lacking.

Another interesting fact connected with Fort McIntosh, was the visit in 1785, of the Commissioners then running the western boundary of Pennsylvania.

On the 25th of August, the joint Commissioners of Virginia and Pennsylvania, consisting of Andrew Ellicott[66] and Joseph Neville,[67] for Virginia, and David Rittenhouse[68] and Andrew Porter,[69] for Pennsylvania, reported that they had finished the meridian line from the, southwest corner of Pennsylvania to the river Ohio, and marked it by cutting a vista over all the principal hills, felling and deadening trees through the lower grounds, and placing stones marked on the east side "P," and on the west side "V," accurately on the meridian line. That part of Virginia on the west side is now known as the "Pan Handle."

Under a resolution of Pennsylvania, of May 5th, 1785, David Rittenhouse, Andrew Porter and Andrew Ellicott, were appointed Commissioners to continue the western boundary, north from the Ohio river, to the northwest corner of the State on Lake Erie.

The Commissioners began their survey from the Ohio, August 23rd, 1785. On the 29th, of August, Messrs. Porter and Ellicott visited Fort McIntosh, by water, and in a few days Dr. McDowell and Major Finney returned the visit. On the 11th of September, the Commissioners were visited also by Col. Harmar and Major Doughty.[70]

The precise time when Fort McIntosh was abandoned by the troops is not known, but from a letter of Col. Harmar, dated October, 22d, 1785, it was probably in November, 1785, the troops then being about to be sent down the Ohio to protect the Treaty Commissioners at the mouths of the Muskingum, Miami and other places.

Among the incidents connected with Fort McIntosh, I have learned that four soldiers were shot for desertion. I have found no record of the execution, yet there seems to be no doubt of the fact, Though true I would prefer not to notice the incident. Desertion in time of war cannot be excused, yet, when we read the letters of Col. Brodhead and Gen'l Irvine, detailing the want, suffering, starvation, and the ragged and abject condition of the men in this department, sympathy for these poor creatures, who suffered the extreme penalty of the law, will arise. The heart yields its better feeling in spite of the necessity.

I am glad I do not know their names to perpetuate their fatal error. It is painful to think that the prosperity we now enjoy has been secured at the expense of so much suffering and distress.

The following report to Congress throws light on Fort McIntosh, and it is also of general interest:

REPORT OF THE DEPARTMENT OF WAR.

Extract from the Journal of Congress.

THURSDAY, OCTOBER 2nd, 1788. The Committee consisting of Mr. Howard, Mr. Few, Mr. Dayton, Mr. Gillman and Mr. Hemington, appointed to make full inquiry into the proceedings of the Department of War, beg leave to report and present to the view of Congress a summary statement of the various branches of the Department of War.[71]

Of the stations occupied by the troops on the frontiers:

FORT FRANKLIN, on French creek, near a post formerly called Venango, is a small strong fort, with one cannon, was erected in 1787, and garrisoned with one company. The excellent construction and execution of this work reflects honor on the abilities and industry of Capt. Heart, who garrisons it with his company and was his own engineer. This post was established for the purpose of defending the frontiers of Pennsylvania, which are much exposed by the facility with which the Indians can cross from Lake Erie, either to French creek, or the Juddaghue Lake, and the Connewango branch, and thence descend the rapid river Allegheny.[72]

FORT PITT has only an officer and a few men to receive the supplies and dispatches forwarded to the troops by the Secretary of War.

FORT MCINTOSH is ordered to be demolished, and a blockhouse to be erected in lieu thereof, a few miles up the Big Beaver Creek, to protect the communication up the same, and also to cover the country.[73]

FORT HARMAR, at the mouth of the Muskingum, is a well constructed fort, with five bastions and three cannon mounted. It is at present garrisoned with four companies; and is considered as headquarters, being conveniently situated to reinforce up or down the river Ohio.

FORT STEUBEN, at the rapids of the Ohio, on the west side, is a well constructed small fort, with one cannon, and is garrisoned with a major and two companies. This post is established to cover the country from the incursions of the Indians, and it serves as a post of communication to Fort Vincennes, on the Wabash.[74]

FORT VINCENNES, on the Wabash, is a work erected during the year 1787, and has four small brass cannon. It is garrisoned by a major and two companies. It is established to curb the incursions of the Wabash Indians into Kentucky county, and to prevent the usurpation of the Federal lands, the fertility of which has been too strong a temptation to the lawless people of the frontiers, who posted themselves there in the year 1786. Brigadier General Harmar, by order of Congress, formed an expedition in August; 1787, for the purpose of dispossessing them, but previous to his arrival, most of the intruders had abandoned their settlements.[75]

The Lake mentioned in this report; and spelled Juddagghue, is evidently Chautauqua. The blockhouse referred to was built on the little stream emptying into the Big Beaver, below New Brighton, still known as "Blockhouse run." This blockhouse was commanded by Lieut. Nathan McDowell, in 1789.

Captain Jonathan Heart, mentioned as having erected Fort Franklin, was a distinguished soldier, a graduate of Yale, with high honors. Beginning at Bunker's Hill, he performed valuable services in the Revolutionary War, and was one of the few officers retained in the service after the close of the war with England. He marched with his company from Connecticut, and reached Fort Pitt October 12th, 1785, keeping a full journal of his march.[76] Soon after, his arrival he was ordered to Fort McIntosh, where he remained with his company, until the 25th of October, when he left for the mouth of the Muskingum, and assisted in building Fort Harmar there. After various services, he was ordered to Franklin, on French Creek.

Although pressed westward, the Indians did not cease their depredations eastward. The Pittsburgh Gazette, of July, 1788, contains a notice by Richard Butler, Superintendent of Indian Affairs, warning the people that some twenty Chippewas and Ottawas had passed Detroit on their way to war.

The Gazette of the same month, states the capture of Col. Joseph Michel and three others, by the Indians, about twenty miles below the Big Miami. Their boat was seized and plundered. They were ransomed by Scotch and French traders from Detroit.

Even so late as July, 1789, the Indians came within two miles of Pittsburgh. The following is from the Gazette of July 2d, 1789:

> Yesterday was brought to this place and buried, the bodies of two young men named Arthur Graham and Alexander Campbell, who had gone out the evening before to fish. They were killed by the savages about two miles from this place.

The Indian war still continued. Generals Harmar and St. Clair were both defeated by the Indians within the Ohio territory, the former in 1790, and the latter in 1791.[77] It was not until the Indians were defeated on the Maumee, by General Anthony Wayne, in 1794, and peace concluded with them by him in 1795, that the Ohio country and Western Pennsylvania became free from their incursions.[78]

General Wayne had encamped with his army in the winter of 1792–3, on the land now of the Harmony Society, below Economy, in Beaver county, his encampment being known as "Legionville." His purpose was to subject his army to strict military discipline, the want of which was believed to be the cause of Harmar and St. Clair's defeats. In April, 1793, he moved his army to Fort Washington,[79] (now Cincinnati,) remaining there until the spring of 1794.

Having related the prominent facts connected with Fort McIntosh and its times, it is proper now to state the circumstances leading to the treaty of the State with the Indians there in January, 1785.

By a treaty made at Fort Stanwix, (now Rome, N. Y.,) on the 5th of November, 1768, between the Penns and the Six Nations, the Indian title was extinguished westward, by lines which became the eastern boundary of the territory included in the next treaty with the Six Nations, made at Fort Stanwix, on the 23d of October, 1784, by Commissioners of the State of Pennsylvania. There were certain tribes in Western Pennsylvania not parties to the treaty of 1784, chiefly Wyandots and Delaware, then actually occupying the western territory. It became necessary in the treaty of October 23, 1784. The treaty of the Pennsylvania Commissioners with the Wyandots and Delawares at Fort McIntosh, terminated in a deed dated January 21, 1785, conveying the Indian title by the same boundaries contained in the treaty of October 23d, 1784, viz:

> Beginning on the south side of the river Ohio, where the western boundary of the State crosses the river, near Shingo's old town, at the mouth of Beaver Creek, and thence by a due north line to the end of the forty-second and beginning of the forty-third degree of north latitude; thence by a due east line separating the forty-second and forty-third degrees of north latitude to the east side of the east branch of the river Susquehanna; thence by the bounds of the late purchase made at Fort Stanwix, the 5th. of November, Anno Domini 1768, as follows: Down the said east branch of the Susquehanna, on the east side thereof, till it comes opposite the mouth of a creek called by the Indian Awandac, and across the river and up said creek, on the south side thereof, all along the range of hills called Burnett's Hills by the English, and ——— by the Indians, on the north side of them to the head of a creek which runs into the west branch of the Susquehanna, which creek is by the Indians called Tyadachton, and by the Pennsylvanians Pine Creek; and down the said creek on the west, side thereof, to the said west branch of the Susquehanna; then crossing the said river and running up the same on the south side thereof, the several courses thereof to the fork of the same river, which lies nearest to a place on the river Ohio, (Allegheny,) called Kittanning, and from the fork by a straight line to Kittanning aforesaid, and then down the said river Ohio, by the several courses thereof, to where the boundary of the said State of Pennsylvania crosses the same, at the place of beginning.

It will be noticed that by this description the western boundary was supposed to cross at the mouth of the Big Beaver. The line as actually run in 1785 was found to cross near the mouth of Little Beaver Creek. This error of position caused difficulty in making the donation surveys.

The fork on the west branch of the Susquehanna from which the line ran directly to Kittanning is known as the Canoe Fork. It is probable that the creek called Awandac by the Indians gave name to Towanda in Bradford county.

The history of the reservation of the 3,000 acres of the State at the mouth of the Big Beaver including Fort McIntosh referred to in General Irvine's instructions to Sergeant Lee and John McClure is this.

The surrender of Cornwallis at Yorktown and the provisional treaty with Great Britain of November 30, 1782, left no doubt of a final treaty of peace. With this expectation, and that of the final extinguishment of the Indian title; the Assembly of Pennsylvania passed the Act of 12th March, 1783. It appropriated the territory north of the Ohio and west of the Allegheny river and Connewango creek, to the use of the soldiers of the Pennsylvania Revolutionary line; the northern part for donations for their services, and the southern for the redemption of the certificates of depreciation from the continental currency, given for their pay. The dividing line ran due west from Mogulbughtitona creek above Kittanning, passing about six or seven miles, south of New Castle, Lawrence county. Out of the southern part, the State reserved to herself two tracts of 3,000 acres each, one at the mouth of the Allegheny river west side, and the other at the mouth of the Big Beaver, including Fort McIntosh. The Beaver reservation was surveyed in April or May, 1785 by Alexander McClain, Esq.[80] This was the prospective survey referred to in General Irvine's instructions to Lee and McClure.

It was on the latter reservation the town and outlots of Beaver were surveyed by Daniel Leet in November, 1792. Owing to the absence of the Commissioners appointed to superintend the survey, the survey of Leet was void, and an Act of confirmation was passed the 6th of March, 1793.

There is a fact locally interesting, connected with the command of Col. Brodhead at Fort McIntosh. He then became acquainted with the Falls of the Big Beaver. These falls, upper, middle and lower, are fifty-two feet altogether, as was ascertained by the United States Engineers, between 1820 and 1830. Col. Brodhead became Surveyor General of Pennsylvania, and on the very day of the passage of the

The Ohio Country, 1783–1800.

59

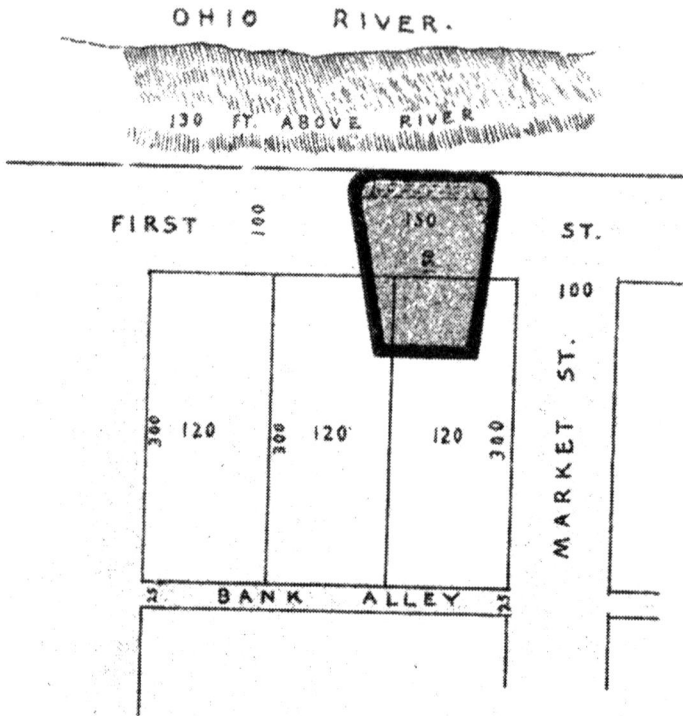

The site of Fort McIntosh in 19th Century Beaver, Pennsylvania as sketched by Daniel Agnew. Reproduced from George Dallas Alberts, *Frontier Forts of Western Pennsylvania,* Vol. II, 1916.

Act of the 3rd of April, 1792, opening these lands to survey and settlement, he took out two warrants for the lands opposite the middle falls, on Walnut Bottom run. On these tracts the town of Beaver Falls now rests. One warrant was in the name of Joseph Williams, on which a survey of 410 acres, and six per cent allowance for roads was made. The other was in the name of William Barker, on which a survey of

440 acres and the allowance was made. The actual content of both was 898 acres. The latter tract came down to a red oak on the west bank of the Beaver about twenty-five yards above the old Fallston dam, and ran up to a black oak, which stood near to where the cotton factory stood. This black oak was the lower corner of the Joseph William's survey. The writer was present at the surveys of these tracts in the year 1833, pending litigation.

Thus we have seen that, almost forgotten by the public, and its site scarcely recognizable now, Fort McIntosh was once a place of note, and the scene of important operations and events. Little over a century has passed, and few now can estimate the change. Then a wilderness where red men roamed and the tomahawk and scalping knife gleamed—now a population of fifty thousand souls fill the small county of Beaver, crowded with mills and factories.

What spot more worthy of a monument than the site of Fort McIntosh?

Notes:

[1] General Lachlan McIntosh (1725–1806) was commander of American forces on the Ohio from May, 1778 until May 1779.

[2] Father René Mésnard (1605–1661), Jesuit missionary; Father Joseph Le Caron (c. 1586–1632); Recollet missionary; Father Claude Allouez (1622–1689), Jesuit missionary; Father Jacques Marquette (1637–1675), Jesuit missionary; Louis Jolliet (1645–1700), explorer; René-Robert Cavelier de la Salle (1643–1687), explorer; Father Louis Hennepin (1626–1705), Recollet missionary; Louis de Buade, Comte de Frontenac et de Palluau (1622–1698), Governor of New France; Samuel de Champlain (d. 1635), founder of Quebec. All were active in exploring the upper Great Lakes and interior of the North America.

[3] Adrien Jolliet, older brother of Louis Jolliet, is believed to be the first European to cross Lake Erie in 1769. He travelled from Lake Huron down the Detroit River into Lake Erie and followed the northern shore to Lake Ontario. Antoine Laumet de Lamothe Cadillac (1658–1730) founded Detroit in 1701.

[4] The French, under the command of Captain Paul Marin de la Malgue (1692–1753), occupied the Allegheny River Valley in 1753. They built Fort Presqu'Île, Fort Rivière aux Boeufs, and Fort Machault. Fort Presqu'Île was at present day Erie, PA, Fort Rivière-aux-boeufs was constructed on the headwaters of French Creek at present-day Waterford, PA, and Fort Machault at the mouth of French Creek at present-day Franklin, PA. Many of the related documents can be found in Fernand Grenier, ed. *Papiers Contrecoeurs et autre documents concernant le conflit Anglo-Français sur l'Ohio de 1745 á 1756,* Quebec: Les presses universitaires Laval, 1952.

[5] La Salle was sent on a mission to discover the Ohio River in 1669–1770. However, it is highly unlikely that he ever actually got anywhere near the Ohio Country. Céline Dupré "René-Robert Cavelier de la Salle," *Dictionary of Canadian Biography,* 1:173-74.

[6] Captain Pierre-Joseph Céloron de Blainville (1693–1759) commanded the expedition which left Montreal on June 15, 1749. They traveled down the Allegheny and Ohio Rivers to the Great Miami, and then upriver to Fort des Miamis near present day Fort Wayne, IN.

[7] Roland-Michel Barrin de la Galissonière, Marquis de la Galissonière (1693–1756), served as commandant general of New France from 1747–1749.

[8] This is incorrect. The French governors of New France ruled from Quebec or Montreal.

[9] Captain Claude-Pierre Pécaudy de Contrecoeur (1705–1775) took command of French forces on the Ohio in 1754. He arrived at the forks of the Ohio on April 17, 1754 and forced the Virginians occupying the spot to withdraw. He immediately began the construction of Fort Duquesne, named after Ange Duquesne de Menneville, Marquis Duquesne (circa 1700 – 1778). Duquesne served as governor of New France 1752–1755.

[10] Conrad Weiser (1696–1760) was often used by the government of Pennsylvania to negotiate with the Indians.

[11] George Croghan (1720–1782) was one of the most influential traders in Pennsylvania. James Hamilton (circa 1718–1783) served as governor of Pennsylvania from 1748–1754 and again from 1759–1768.

[12] Robert Dinwiddie (1692–1770) was lieutenant governor of Virginia from 1751–1758. He took a leading roll in combating the French occupation of the Ohio Valley.

[13] Christopher Gist (1706–1759) served as Washington's guide on his mission to the French forts.

[14] Colonel Joshua Fry (1700–1754) was commander of the Virginia Regiment. He died on May 31, 1754 from injuries suffered when he was thrown from his horse. Agnew incorrectly identifies Edward Ward as a lieutenant. He was actually commissioned an ensign in Captain William Trent's company of the Virginia Regiment. He was in command of the detachment of Virginians occupying the forks of the Ohio when Contrecoeur arrived on April 17, 1754. Ward served as a lieutenant and then a captain in the Pennsylvania forces later in the war.

[15] Ensign Joseph Coulon de Villiers de Jumonville (1718–1754) commanded the small French detachment sent to demand the withdrawal of Washington's force. Jumonville was killed on a surprise attack commanded by Washington at Jumonville Glen, PA, on May 28, 1754. Jumonville's brother Captain Louis Coulon de Villiers (1710–1757) commanded the French force that defeated Washington at the Battle of Great Meadows, or Fort Necessity, on July 3, 1754.

[16] Captain Jacob Van Braam (1725–1784), who served as interpreter, was accused by many of deliberately misinterpreting the meaning of the French word *"l'assassinat."* He was later exonerated. The Terms of Capitulation can be found in W. W. Abbott, et. al., eds. *The Papers of George Washington: Colonial Series,* Charlotte, VA: University Press of Virginia, 1983-1995, 1:165–67. The quote is from a letter by Major Adam Stephen (1718–1791), printed in the *Maryland Gazette* on August 19, 1754.

[17] A British Army that included the 44th and 48th Regiments of Foot, under the command of Major General Edward Braddock (1694–1755) was defeated at the Battle of Monongahela on July 9, 1755.

[18] General John Forbes (1707–1759) was commander of the expedition. Major James Grant (1720–1806) of the 77th Highlanders, led an unsuccessful raid against Fort Duquesne on September 14, 1758.

[19] Major General Sir Jeffery Amherst (1717–1797) was commander-in-chief of British forces in North America 1758–1797. Governor Pierre de Rigaud de Vaudreuil de Cavagnial, Marquis de Vaudreuil (1698–1778), surrendered all of New France to Amherst at Montreal on September 8, 1760.

[20] Pontiac (d. 1769), war chief of the Ottawa at Detroit, held a secret council at Rivière à l'Écorce, south of Detroit, on April 27, 1763.

[21] Colonel Henry Bouquet (1719–1765) defeated the Indians at the Battle of Bushy Run on August 6, 1763.

[22] Major Daniel Leet (1748–1830) had served as a quartermaster, paymaster, and brigade major during the War of American Independence. He also served as second-in-command on William Crawford's disastrous expedition against the Ohio Indians in 1782. After the war he settled on Chartier's Creek and became surveyor in Western Pennsylvania. Leet also served in the General Assembly of Pennsylvania in 1791–1792.

[23] Governor John Murray, 4th Earl Dunmore (1732–1809) led the war against the Ohio Indians in 1774. The Indians, led by the Shawnee chief, Wynepuechsika, or Cornstalk (circa 1720–1777), were defeated at the Battle of Point Pleasant on October 10. Dunmore then marched up the valley of the Scioto River and forced the Indians to sue for peace.

[24] Captain John Neville (1731–1803) eventually rose to the rank of brigadier general and, as inspector of revenue, figured prominently in the Whiskey Rebellion of 1794.

[25] Brigadier General Edward Hand (1744–1802), a veteran of Bunker Hill, commanded at Fort Pitt 1777–1780. He was appointed adjutant general of the Continental Army in 1781.

[26] Simon Girty (1741–1818), Matthew Elliot (1739–1814), and Alexander McKee (circa 1735–1799), were all active Indian agents at Fort Pitt. They fled to Detroit to serve the British in March, 1777. Simon's brothers James Girty (1743–1817) and George Girty (1746–1796) also acted as British Indian agents during the War of American Independence and afterwards.

[27] Henry Hamilton (circa 1734–1796) served as lieutenant governor of Detroit from 1775 until his capture by George Rogers Clark at Fort Vincennes on February 25, 1779. While Hamilton was certainly a proponent of using Indians against the colonial frontier, there is no concrete evidence that he ever purchased scalps. See Elizabeth Arthur, "Henry Hamilton," *Dictionary of Canadian Biography,* 4:321–25

[28] George Bryan (1731–1791) was vice-president of the supreme executive council of Pennsylvania 1777 and became president of the supreme executive council in 1778.

[29] Fort Laurens was built at present-day Coshocton, OH in December, 1778. It was abandoned in August 1779. Henry Laurens (1724–1792) of South Carolina was president of the Continental Congress from November 1777 to December 1778.

[30] Colonel Daniel Brodhead (1736–1809) of the 8th Pennsylvania Regiment arrived at Fort Pitt as second-in-command in March, 1778. He succeeded McIntosh as commander at Fort Pitt in April, 1779 and served in that capacity until 1781. Colonel John Gibson (1740–1822) served as commander at Fort Laurens and second-in-command on the Ohio. He was an opponent of Brodhead and suc-

ceeded him as commander on the Ohio in 1781. He was later appointed secretary of the Territory of Indiana in 1801, and served as acting governor of the State of Indiana from 1811–1813.

[31] Major General John Armstrong (1717–1795).

[32] General Nathanael Greene (1742–1786).

[33] Arthur Lee (1740–1792), youngest son of Thomas Lee, had served as agent in London for the colony of Massachusetts prior to the war. He was appointed commissioner to France in 1776 and Spain in 1777. Lee served in the Continental Congress 1782–1784.

[34] Brigadier General Richard Butler was commissioner of Indian affairs as well as a commissioner at the treaty negotiations at Fort McIntosh in 1784. He commanded the right wing of General St. Clair's Army in 1791 and was killed at St. Clair's defeat on November 4, 1791. Colonel Josiah Harmar (1753–1813) was named commander of 1st American Regiment at Fort Pitt and Fort McIntosh, June, 1784.

[35] Archibald Lochry (1733–1781) was County Lieutenant of Westmoreland County, Pennsylvania. He led a detachment of about 100 militia down the Ohio in 1781 to join up with George Rogers Clark for a proposed expedition against Detroit. The British and Native Americans ambushed his party near the mouth of present-day Laughery Creek in Dearborn County, IN on August 24. Lochry was killed and his entire detachment was either killed or taken prisoner.

[36] Captain John Clark (d. 1819) had served as an aide-de-camp to General Nathanael Greene. He was transferred to the 8th Pennsylvania Regiment on July 1, 1778 and served until the end of the war. He rejoined the army in 1791 and was wounded in St. Clair's defeat of November 4, 1791. He later rose to the rank of colonel. See Louise Phelps Kellogg, *Frontier Advance on the Upper Ohio, 1778–1779,* Madison, WI: State Historical Society of Wisconsin, 1916, p. 205.

[37] Joseph Reed (1741–1785) was president of the supreme executive council of Pennsylvania 1778–1781.

[38] Dr. John Connolly (b. 1750) was a native of Pennsylvania and nephew of George Croghan. A western land speculator, he governed Pittsburgh on behalf of Virginia, 1773–1775. Connolly fled the country with Lord Dunmore at the outbreak of war in 1775.

[39] Captain Samuel Brady (1756–1795) of the 8th Pennsylvania Regiment later served as a scout. He commanded the scouts under General Anthony Wayne in 1792. See Kellogg, *Frontier Advance,* 158–59.

[40] Major George Slaughter (1739–1818) of the 12th Virginia Regiment, arrived at Fort Pitt in April 1780 while en route to join George Rogers Clark in Kentucky. He later became lieutenant colonel of all Virginia forces in Kentucky. Slaughter served on the Virginia Assembly in 1784. See Kellogg, *Frontier Advance,* 179–80.

[41] Colonel Timothy Pickering (1745–1829) of Massachusetts was a veteran of the Battle of Lexington. He served as quarter master general of the Continental Army from August 1780 to July 1785.

[42] Captain Thomas McIntyre commanded an independent company in Western Pennsylvania until May, 1782.

[43] Colonel David Shepherd (1734–1795) was County Lieutenant of Ohio County, VA.

[44] Brigadier General William Irvine (1741–1804) commanded at Fort Pitt from September 1781 to October 1783.

[45] The expedition against Detroit proposed by Brigadier General George Rogers Clark (1752–1818) never departed from its rendezvous point due to a lack of men and attacks by Native American warriors.

[46] Captain Isaac Craig (1742–1826) arrived at Fort Pitt in April 1780. He commanded the artillery bound for Clark's expedition. Craig was promoted to major in December 1781. He settled in Pittsburgh after the war and became a prominent businessman. He helped found the first glass factory west of the Allegheny Mountains in 1791.

[47] William Lee and John McClure were both sergeants in the 8th Pennsylvania Regiment. Lee served in the company of Captain Basil Prather and McClure served in Captain John Finley's company.

[48] John Dickinson (1732–1808) served as president of the supreme executive council of Pennsylvania from 1782–1785. He afterwards spent many years in Delaware politics and signed the United States Constitution as a delegate from Delaware.

[49] Captain David Ziegler (1748–1811) and Captain William McCurdy (1728–1822) were both veterans of the War of American Independence and were commissioned to command companies from Pennsylvania in the First American Regiment. Zeigler was promoted to major in 1790. He was later elected the first mayor of Cincinnati, OH in 1802 and became adjutant-general of Ohio in 1807. McCurdy served as a captain on the frontier from 1784–1791.

[50] Colonel Alexander Lowry (1723–1805) was well known to the tribes of Ohio. He had been a highly successful trader on the frontier since the 1740s. He later served as a Pennsylvania State Senator from Lancaster.

[51] Samuel J. Atlee (1739–1786) had served as colonel of the Pennsylvania Musketry Battalion until he was taken prisoner at the Battle of Long Island in 1776. He served in the Continental Congress from 1778–1782. Colonel Francis Johnston (1748–1815) had commanded the 5th Pennsylvania Regiment during the War of American Independence.

[52] Fort Harmar was at the mouth of the Muskingum River at present-day Marietta, OH. Lieutenant Colonel Josiah Harmar ordered its construction in October 1785. It served as army headquarters from 1785–1788 and was occupied until 1795.

[53] Duncan and Finley had both been traders on the Ohio frontier for several years. Finley is said to have been present at the Battle of Monongahela on July 9, 1755. See Charles A. Hanna, *The Wilderness Trail, or the Ventures and Adventures of the Pennsylvania Traders on the Allegheny Path,* 2 Volumes, New

York: G. P. Putnam's Sons, 1911. For John Prentice see 2:378. For Hanna's discussion of John Findley see volume 2, chapter 7.

[54] Captain Walter Finney (1747–1820) was taken prisoner at the Battle of Long Island in 1776. He later served as a captain in the 6th Pennsylvania Regiment. He was commissioned a captain in the First American Regiment on August 12, 1784 and commanded at Fort McIntosh for a short time until Harmar arrived. He was serving as a major when he resigned his commission on September 1, 1787. Finney later served as a judge in Chester County, PA from 1790–1820.

[55] Thomas Douglass was captain of the 2nd Artillery Company, First American Regiment, in 1784–85. He has served in the 1st Pennsylvania Artillery during the war.

[56] Lieutenant Joseph Ashton had served in the 1st Pennsylvania Artillery during the American War of Independence. He was now serving in the 2nd Artillery Company.

[57] Lieutenant Herbert Stewart (1754–1795) had been commissioned an ensign in the 12th Pennsylvania Regiment on October 16, 1776. He was promoted to 2nd lieutenant on May 1, 1777 and then to 1st lieutenant on January 9, 1778. He was transferred to the 6th Pennsylvania on July 1, 1778 and was wounded and taken prisoner at Green Springs, VA on July 6, 1781. He was commissioned 1st lieutenant and adjutant of the First American Regiment on August 12, 1784.

[58] Erkuries Beatty (1759–1823) served in the ranks at the Battle of White Plains and was a sergeant at Long Island in 1776. He was promoted to ensign in the 4th Pennsylvania Regiment on January 3, 1777 and 1st lieutenant on May 2, 1777. Beatty was wounded at the Battle of Germantown. He was appointed 1st lieutenant in the First American Regiment on July 24, 1784 and served as paymaster for the western army 1786–1788. He commanded the garrison at Fort St. Vincent, 1789–1790. Beatty was promoted to major of the 5th Regiment of infantry in 1792 and resigned from the army in 1793.

[59] Thomas Doyle was commissioned lieutenant in the First American Regiment on August 12, 1784. He was serving as a captain in 1794 when he was sent by General Anthony Wayne to built Fort Massac at present-day Metropolis, IL.

[60] John Armstrong (1755–1816) had served in the 3rd and 12th Pennsylvania Regiments. He served in the West from 1784–1793, stationed at Fort Pitt, 1785–1786 and at Fort Finney, 1786–1790. Armstrong also explored the lower Missouri and Wabash River Valleys in 1790. He fought with Harmar in 1790 and St. Clair in 1791. On retiring in 1793, Armstrong operated a store near Cincinnati, OH until 1807. He also served at treasurer of the Northwest Territory from 1796–1802. Armstrong died in Clark County, IN. His papers are held by the Indiana Historical Society. See their web site at www.indianahistory.org for reference.

[61] Ebenezer Denny (1761–1822) had served as a dispatch rider between Carlisle and Fort Pitt. He also served a short time on a privateer in the Caribbean before accepting a commission in the Pennsylvania line in 1780 and kept a diary of the

Yorktown campaign. He then served in the First American Regiment from 1784–1791 rising to the rank of major. He compiled a glossary of the Delaware and Shawnee Indian languages while serving at Fort McIntosh in 1785. He later settled in Pittsburgh, became a banker, and was elected mayor in 1816.

[62] Nathan McDowell, from Pennsylvania, was a signatory of the treaty with the Shawnee at the mouth of the Great Miami River in January 1786. He served under Harmar on the Wabash in 1787 and accompanied him on his trip to Kaskaskia, IL. McDowell was in command at the Big Beaver Blockhouse at present-day New Brighton, PA in 1789.

[63] Dr. John McDowell (1745–1825) had served as an officer and surgeon in the 2nd Pennsylvania and 6th Pennsylvania Regiments from 1776–1783. He then served as surgeon of the First American Regiment from 1784–1788. He was residing in Greensburg, PA when he died.

[64] Dr. Richard Allison (1757–1816) had served as surgeon's mate in the 5th Pennsylvania Regiment. He succeeded McDowell as surgeon of the First Infantry Regiment in 1788. He was promoted to surgeon of the general staff in 1792 and served until 1796. He later became the first physician in Cincinnati, OH. See Mary C. Gillett, *The Army Medical Department, 1775–1818,* United States Army Historical Series, Washington DC: U.S. Government Printing Office, 1981.

[65] Colonel Joseph Wood (1712–1791) was born in Pennsylvania and moved to Georgia in 1774. He was severely wounded while serving in Canada in 1776. Wood commanded the 2nd Pennsylvania Battalion and then the 3rd Pennsylvania Regiment. He resigned his commission and returned to Georgia in 1776. Wood served as a delegate from Georgia to the Continental Congress in 1777–1778.

[66] Andrew Ellicot (1754–1820) was a highly regarded surveyor and astronomer and was appointed surveyor general of the United States in 1792. In 1797 he surveyed the boundary between the United States and Spanish Florida. In 1803 he trained Meriweather Lewis to survey in preparation for his exploration of the Louisiana Territory. In 1811 he surveyed the northern boundary of Georgia. In his later years he taught mathematics at West Point, where he died in 1820.

[67] Joseph Neville (1730–1819) had served in the House of Burgesses for Hampshire County, 1773–1776. He also served in the Virginia Conventions of 1775 and 1776. In 1782 he helped complete the survey of the Mason-Dixon Line. He was appointed surveyor of Hampshire County, VA in 1784. He served in the United States Congress from 1793–1795 and died in Moorefield, WV.

[68] David Rittenhouse (1732–1796) was a well-known surveyor, mathematician, inventor, and astronomer, and a member of the American Philosophical Society. He invented the Rittenhouse compass, used by surveyors until the mid-nineteenth century. He had helped complete the Mason-Dixon Line in 1784. He later acted as the first director of the United States Mint, 1792–1795.

[69] Andrew Porter (1743–1813) had taught mathematics in Philadelphia prior to the War of Independence. He was commissioned a captain of marines in 1776

but soon transferred to the artillery. Porter fought at Princeton, Brandywine, Germantown, and on Sullivan's expedition, and had risen to the rank of colonel of the 4th Pennsylvania Artillery by the end of the war. Porter was later commissioned major general of Pennsylvania militia and served as surveyor general of the United States 1809–1813.

[70] John Doughty (1754–1826) joined the New Jersey artillery in 1776. He served as aide-de-camp to General Schuyler at Saratoga in 1777. He was appointed fort major of West Point in 1782. In 1785 he was sent to Fort McIntosh. He resigned from the army in 1792 but again served as lieutenant colonel of the 2nd Regiment of Artillery and Engineers 1798–1800. He died in Morristown, NJ.

[71] John Eagar Howard (1752–1827) of Maryland, William Few (1748–1828) of Georgia, Jonathan Dayton (1760–1824) of New Jersey, and Nicholas Gilman (1755–1814) of New Hampshire were all members of the Continental Congress in 1788.

[72] Captain Jonathan Heart (1748–1791) served in the First American Regiment 1785–1791. He is probably best known for his description of the Native American mounds at Marietta, OH in 1791. He was killed at St. Clair's Defeat, November 4, 1791, on the banks of the Wabash River near present-day Fort Recovery, OH. Fort Franklin, at Franklin, PA was garrisoned from 1787 until 1796.

[73] A garrison was maintained at Big Beaver Blockhouse from 1788 until approximately 1793.

[74] Fort Steuben was constructed at present-day Steubenville, OH in 1786. It was destroyed by fire in 1790 and the site was abandoned.

[75] The fort at Vincennes, actually named Fort Knox, was built on the north side of present-day Buntin Street in Vincennes, IN. The fort was moved three miles above the town in 1803.

[76] Butterfield, C. W., ed., *Journal of Capt. Jonathan Heart on the march with his company from Connecticut to Fort Pitt, in Pittsburgh, Pennsylvania, from the Seventh of September to the Twelfth of October, 1785, Inclusive: To Which Is Added the Dickinson-Harmar Correspondence of 1784–5,* Albany, NY: J. Munsell's Sons, 1885.

[77] Josiah Harmar and Arthur St. Clair both led armies that were defeated by Native American forces led by the Miami chief Michikinakoua, or Little Turtle (c. 1747–1812). Harmar's invading force was defeated on October 22, 1790 at the forks of the Maumee River in present-day Fort Wayne, IN. St. Clair was defeated on November 4, 1791 near the present site of Fort Recovery, OH.

[78] Major General "Mad" Anthony Wayne (1745–1796) defeated the forces of Michikinakoua on the Maumee River at the Battle of Fallen Timbers on August 20, 1793. Per the terms of the Treaty of Greenville, signed on August 3, 1795, the Native Americans ceded most of the lands in southern Ohio and Indiana to the United States.

[79] Fort Washington, at present-day Cincinnati, OH, was built in 1789. A garrison was maintained there until 1803.

[80] Alexander McClean (1746–1834) was a well-known surveyor from Uniontown, PA. He had led the survey that completed the Mason-Dixon Line in 1782.

"Fort Pitt"

AND ITS TIMES.

A HISTORICAL SKETCH

BY DANIEL AGNEW, LL. D.

Originally Published:

Pittsburgh
Myers, Skinkle & Co., Printers, Stationers, Binders.
1894.

"Fort Pitt"
and Its Times

FORT PITT! Two little words—life seeds. What do they import? A growth no fancy could then conceive, or imagination clothe with reality. Let a radius of five miles be drawn around the Pittsburgh Point, and its area contains five hundred thousand souls. Let the radii be produced, and the circle includes a grand country supporting a population of sixty-five millions, and land to spare. Unless, like myself, one had seen Pittsburgh only half grown, he cannot realize that one hundred and forty years ago; in the year 1753; Washington stood at the junction of the rivers, in a wild and lonely region, surrounded only by unbroken forest, tangled vine and wild grass untrodden, except by the savage and the ferocious beast.

Where now is Grant's Hill, once the scene of warfare and slaughter? The big toe of a long hill range, in my youth it came down to Fourth avenue, almost reaching Smithfield street, and at Ross street crossing Fourth, and descending, its foot nearly reached Third avenue. On its northern side it presented a steep declivity, with a large pond at the foot, extending rather diagonally from a point between Diamond street and Fourth avenue, to Seventh avenue.

The plateau top, then the scene of militia musters, the playground of boys, and the walk of amorous swains and early belles, is no longer seen, but cut away, excavated, and sloped to gentle descent, it now challenges neither eye nor muscle, but full of houses, churches and buildings; the youth of to-day would believe himself trifled with, if told that the writer saw it as described. The only evidence it now presents to the Pittsburgher of its former self is the steeper grade on Fifth avenue, called the "Hump."

The purpose of this humble effort is to call back the early scene, following the visit of Washington, and recreate a vision of "Fort Pitt," made alas, too dim by intervening years, and appealing to the eye, like the outlines of a view embosomed in mist.

It is unnecessary to repeat here the course of events which brought France and England together, in arms, at the junction of the rivers. Those desiring to read an account of it, will find it in the sketch of "Fort McIntosh and its Times," by the writer.

The visit of Washington to the French forts, in 1753, proved that France claimed and intended to hold the entire west to the head of the Ohio, by force of arms, if necessary. The report of Washington to Governor Dinwiddie, of Virginia, led him to send a meagre force to take possession of the junction and build a small fort. The French, warned by these signs, proceeded at once, in 1754, to meet the danger, by sending down the Allegheny, a large force of French and Indians, with cannon, taking possession, and driving away Lieut. Ward, then engaged at work on the Virginia fort. To secure this important position, commanding the rivers and adjacent territory, they proceeded to build a strong work, called by them Du Quesne, after the name of the French Governor-General. This post they held until November, 1758, in the meantime defeating a Virginia force under Washington, compelling him to retreat to Fort Necessity and surrender there; and also, on the 9th day of July, 1755, defeating a large army under General Braddock, composed chiefly of British regulars, commanded by some of her finest officers.

Great Britain, now fairly embarked in war with France, determined to drive the French from Du Quesne and the Ohio. In the year 1758, she sent by the Pennsylvania route a well appointed army under General John Forbes. Upon his near approach, alarmed by the formidable force, the French, late in November (24th) evacuated Fort Du Quesne, setting fire to it, and leaving it largely in ruin.

General John Forbes was a British soldier, of Scottish birth. Educated as a physician, he abandoned his profession to enter the army, serving in the German wars with credit, and was appointed Brigadier-General in America in 1757. In the autumn of 1758, he was appointed to the command of the army sent against Fort Du Quesne. At Raystown, on the Juniata, he became too unwell to travel, and was carried forward on a litter, still commanding his force with a clear intellect and iron will. His disease was consumption, of which he soon died after his return to Philadelphia. Just sixty days after the capture of Du Quesne, William Pitt, the English minister, in a letter dated at Whitehall, January 23, 1759, enclosed in orders to General Sir Jeffery Amherst, Commander-in-Chief of the British Forces in America, wrote to Governor Denny of Pennsylvania, as follows:[1]

I am now to acquaint you that the King has been pleased, immediately upon receiving the account of the success of his arms on the river Ohio, to direct the Commander-in-Chief of his Majesty's forces in North America and Brigadier-General Forbes, to lose no time executing the properest and speediest means for completely restoring, if possible, the ruined Fort Du Quesne to a defensible and respectable state; or by erecting another in the room of it, of sufficient strength, and every way adequate to the great importance of the several objects of maintaining his Majesty's subjects in the undisputed possession of the Ohio; of effectually cutting off the trade and communication this way, between Canada, and the western and southern Indians; of protecting the British Colonies from the incursions to which they have been exposed since the French built the above fort, and thereby made themselves masters of the navigation of the Ohio; and of fixing again the several Indian nations in their alliance with and dependence upon his Majesty's government. And the Province under your command is so particularly and nearly interested in the speedy execution of this great and salutary work, that it will be matter of no small surprise, and must reflect the greatest blame on their conduct, should they in any point fail to assist, to the utmost, the King's officers, who shall be employed on this occasion. I have therefore the King's command to signify to you his pleasure, that you should use your utmost endeavors with your Councils and Assembly, to induce them to exert every means in their power for collecting and forwarding the materials of all sorts, and the workmen which shall be wanted, which the Commander-in-Chief in North America, or Brigadier-General Forbes shall require for the service; and that your Province do also furnish every assistance of men, cattle, carriages, provisions, &c., that shall be necessary for the support and maintenance of the King's forces that shall be employed in this essential work, as well as all further operations to be undertaken in these parts the ensuing campaign.

This letter evinces so clearly the British policy, the exactions of the Province, and the severe rule of the King, it is given at length, that those of the present day may perceive the burdens under which their ancestors labored, which with other grievances finally led to revolution. Governor William Denny, to whom the letter was addressed, was only Lieutenant or Deputy Governor under the Penn's, the proprietors of the Province. In obeying the King's commands, he had frequent tilts with the Assembly, even then imbued with the spirit of independence.

This letter was received by General Amherst with his dispatches from Secretary Pitt, and sent by him to Governor Denny on the 28th of March, 1759. In his letter to the Governor, after reciting the contents of Mr. Pitt's letter to the Governor, a copy of which had been sent to him, he expressed the hope that the directions will meet with vigorous and speedy execution, and closes by saying:

And as I have already signified to you that I had appointed Brigadier-General Stanwix[2] to succeed Brigadier-General Forbes in the command to the southward, and desired you to correspond and co-operate with him in every matter relative to the service in those parts, I am now to request you, that all aid and assistance required of you by Mr. Secretary Pitt's within letter, in favor of the late Brigadier-General Forbes, may be granted to Brigadier-General Stanwix, to enable him, in the most expeditious manner to execute the before mentioned great and salutary work, or any other that may be found necessary for the good of the service; and that you would look upon whatever he may ask or require of your Province during his continuance in that command, as coming from myself.

The letter of General Amherst conveying the appointment of General Stanwix, is dated March 18th, 1859, and he was directed to enter on his duties at once.

Sir Jeffery Amherst was a British soldier, whose services in America commenced in 1758. At the recommendation of William Pitt, he was commissioned as Major-General, to co-operate in the reduction of Canada. This he did with great success. In 1760, he was raised to the Peerage, as Lord Amherst, and in the same year was made Governor-General of the British Possessions in America.

General Forbes, when returning to Philadelphia, had left Col. Hugh Mercer,[3] who had been brought from Fort Ligonier with his troops, in command at the ruins of Fort Du Quesne, the chief part of the army returning with General Forbes. The ruinous condition of that fort, and the approaching winter, made a temporary shelter necessary to protect the troops against the severity of the season, and against the French and unfriendly Indians. Accordingly, in December, 1758, a small square stockade with bastions was erected near the bank of the Monongahela river.

On the 8th of January, 1759, Col. Mercer, writing from the fort to Governor Denny, said:

> The intelligence from every quarter makes it evident the French have not yet lost hope of securing a post here. They are extremely busy in collecting the over the Lake Indians, and propose assembling them near Kuskuskee. For this purpose they are now forming magazines of arms and provisions near that place. They have as yet many friends among the Delawares and Shawanese, as appears by Our not receiving the least in formation of this design, though it is formed in the heart of the Delaware country, and these scoundrels come in shoals every day to live upon us, pretending the utmost friendship.

Kuskuskee was an Indian town on the west bank of the Big Beaver, just below the mouth of the Mahoning.

In the same letter, Col. Mercer referred to the alarm of the Six Nations, lest Fort Pitt should be abandoned, leaving them to the hostility of a powerful confederacy of Indians over the Lake, set on by the French; and referred also to the great demand for Indian goods, and a fair trade needed to begin soon. The garrison, he said, consisted of two hundred and eighty men, and was capable of some defence, though huddled up in a hasty manner.

With this letter he sent the proceedings of a council held with the Indians in January, 4th to 8th. They were chiefs of the Six Nations, Shawanese and Delawares. The Chiefs of the Six Nations claimed to be friendly, but said privately the Delawares and Shawanese were not to be depended upon. They expressed great fear of the French, who were near to them. They also desired Col. Mercer not to regard what they might say in the public meeting when the Delawares and Shawanese were present, and protested thoroughly against the abandonment of Fort Pitt. Col. Mercer held several meetings with the Indians, the proceedings of which were forwarded to the Governor.

On the 17th of March, 1759, he reported at the Fort 418 effective rank and file, and on the 4th of April, 409 men; and artillery, two royal howitzers, five cohorns, and a proportion of shot, grapeshot and shells.

General Amherst having at an early day called the attention of the Governor and Assembly to the necessity of a sufficient appropriation, to enable him to execute the King's orders for building a fort at Du Quesne; the Assembly brought in a supply bill for 100,000 pounds. This bill contained a provision for taxing the estates of the Penns. On its being presented to Governor Denny, April 5th, 1759, he declined to give his assent to it on account of the tax upon the estates of the proprietaries, stating his positive orders from them to prevent injury to their property. This led to an acrimonious controversy between the Governor and the Assembly, which was not ended until General Amherst intervened, by informing the Governor he had stated to the Assembly, that if the supply bill failed, he should give over the intended offensive operations, and the building of the fort. The Assembly, however, persisted in their determination to tax the Penns, and he therefore asked the Governor, for the good of the cause, to give his assent to the bill, notwithstanding the instructions of the Penns. The Governor finally consented, and on the 17th of April, returned the bill to the House, saying he would sign it when engrossed and compared. The bill was signed, on which the Speaker, in the name of the House, presented the Governor with an order on the Loan Office for 1,000 pounds.

A fresh controversy soon arose over a bill for a further supply of 50,000 pounds. The bill passed between the Governor and the Assembly so often, it seemed doomed to endless dispute, and led at last to a difference between the Governor and the Colonial Council, but was finally signed by the Governor. Again the House presented him with an order for 1,000 pounds.

Now another controversy arose. Without impressment of wagons and horses, it was impossible to procure them. General Stanwix applied to the Governor for relief, and the Governor besought the Assembly for an Act conferring authority to impress. Nothing was done however. On the 7th day of July, 1759, the Governor laid before the Assembly another letter from General Stanwix, in which he said:

> For God's sake press the Assembly for the same law as last years, with the penalty of twenty pounds; though it be for four or five months, it will be of infinite use to us.

But the General had to leave with the means he had. Several other letters came from General Stanwix on the same subject. On the 16th of August, 1759, he wrote from Fort Bedford,[4] begging the Assembly to pass the law desired, saying without it the campaign would probably be the last, as it could not be carried on, not having yet one-half of the wagons wanted.

Thus the spirit of freedom and independence, even in this straight, was exercising its power over the Colonists, who resisted what they believed, correctly or incorrectly, to be the unjust refusal of the Penns to be taxed for the public safety, and the intolerable exactions of the King in his quarrel with France.

As a consequence of the many obstacles he encountered, General Stanwix did not reach the Fort until late in August, 1759. The new Fort was commenced on the 10th of September, 1759, and was not finished until the 21st of March, 1760. Hugh Henry Brackenridge is authority for saying it cost the British Government about 60,000 pounds. It was called Fort Pitt and Pittsburgh while under the command of Col. Mercer, who dated his letters, some at Fort Pitt and others at Pittsburgh. The Indian conferences during his time were also headed as held at Pittsburgh.

In the interval before the arrival of General Stanwix, Col. Mercer continued in command. On the 9th of July, 1759, he held an important council with the Indians, of whom a large number were in attendance. The following persons were present:

George Croghan, Esq., Deputy Agent to the Honorable William
    Johnson, Baronet.[5]
Col. Hugh Mercer, Commandant at Pittsburgh.
Captains Waggoner, Woodward, Prentice, Morgan, Smallman,
    Clayton, Ward.[6]
Lieutenants Matthews, Hydler, Biddle, Conrad, Kennedy, Sumner,
    Anderson, Hutchins, Dangerfield, Wright.[7]
Ensigns Crawford, Crawford, Morgan.[8]
Messrs. Vixan, Ormsby, Aden, Lightfoot.[9]
Captain Wm. Kent, Captain Thomas McKee,[10] Assistants to George
    Croghan, Esq.

Indians present:

Six Nations: nine chiefs and sixteen warriors.
Delaware Chiefs and Captains, with a great number of others.
Shawanese: three chiefs and fourteen warriors.
Deputies, representing their own and eight other Nations.[11]

The purpose of these councils was to attach the Indians to the British.

Notwithstanding these councils, the bad intentions the Indians, referred to by Col. Mercer, in a former letter to Governor Denny, were now confirmed by a letter from George Croghan to the Governor, dated at Pittsburgh July 15th, 1759. He learned by spies, sent to Venango that seven hundred French, and four hundred Indians were marching from Presque Isle, (Erie,) to Venango. Other Indians joined them there, to the number of five hundred and fifty. While at Venango, the French commandant received a letter which he said contained bad news, informing him that a large English army, and Sir William Johnson, with his Six Nations, were on the march to attack Fort Niagara. The French officer gave immediate orders to return up French Creek, with the artillery and provisions. The spies saw them set off on their return.[12]

On the 6th of August, 1759, Col. Mercer informed the Governor that, owing to so many Indians there, and the expense of provisions, he had been obliged to reduce the garrison to 350 men, and even this number this number could not save an ounce between convoys.

Also, that trouble with the Indians was likely, and small parties lay about Fort Ligonier[13] and Fort Pitt as spies, occasionally taking a scalp or a prisoner. He informed the Governor that Captain Gordon, Chief Engineer, had arrived, with many artificers, and they were preparing materials for building, waiting the coming of the General.[14]

On the 13th day of August, Col. Mercer wrote to the Governor that the garrison was not yet reinforced; the convoys of provisions came in so slowly, that, though small in numbers, they were scarcely supplied from one to another.

General Stanwix having reached the Fort late in August, and commenced the construction of the new Fort as before stated, continued in command until the following spring. On the 24th of October, he held a conference with the Indians in the presence of the army officers, Geo. Croghan, the Deputy, and others. Captain Henry Montour was the interpreter. The Indians were informed that the British had taken Quebec, and that, the French would soon be driven from America. The conference continued on the 25th and 26th of October.

Captain Henry Montour, the interpreter, was a half-breed Indian, the son of a French woman, Catharine Montour, who married a chief of one of the Six Nations. She was said to be the daughter of Count De Frontenac, Governor of New France, and possibly was herself a half-breed. Another account is given of his parentage, but the difference is not so great as to make it important to trace it, the writer of the account describing him as a man of information and education, "but a great savage." As an interpreter, he was of great service. Henry Montour was also known by the name of Andrew, for whose services a tract of land was granted called "Montour's Reserve," at the junction of the Loyalsock with the west branch of the Susquehanna. He was a claimant also of the Island in the Ohio, six miles below Pittsburgh, variously known as Montours, Nevilles, and Long Island.[15]

Immediately on finishing the new Fort, General Stanwix left for Philadelphia, March 21st, 1760, with an escort of 35 chiefs of the Ohio Indians, and 50 men of the Royal American Battallion. When he left, the force at the Fort consisted of 150 Virginians, 150 Pennsylvanians, and 400 of the First Battallion of Royal Americans, under the command of Major Tullikens.[16] Soon after reaching

Philadelphia, he sailed for England, and reached London in the last of July, 1760.

Brigadier John Stanwix was a British soldier, born in England. He rose from a Captaincy of Grenadiers to the command of the First Battallion of the 60th or Royal American Regiment. His headquarters after he came to America were at Carlisle, Pennsylvania, and he was appointed Brigadier-General in December, 1757. In 1758, he built Fort Stanwix, named after himself, on the spot now the site of Rome, New York. Fort Stanwix was the scene of two memorable Pennsylvania treaties with the Indians in 1768 and 1784. In 1759, he returned to Pennsylvania, and was commissioned Major-General, and in the fall of that year built the new Fort Pitt, and was relieved by General Robert Monckton on the 4th of May, 1760. After his return to England, he rose rapidly, and served in Parliament but unfortunately, with his wife and daughter, met his death by shipwreck, in 1767, in crossing the Irish Channel.

General Monckton, who succeeded him, arrived at Fort Pitt to take command June 29th, 1760.[17] Soon after his arrival a large part of the force at the Fort was detached to march towards Presque Isle, (Erie,) in order to join in the reduction of Canada, then threatened by a large force of British. Four companies of the Royal Americans, under Col. Bouquet, and Captain Neill's company of the "Brig" Regiment, left on the 7th of July. On the Wednesday following, Col. Mercer, with three companies of the Pennsylvania regiment, under Captains Biddle, Clapham and Anderson, and two days later two other companies of the same regiment, under Captains Atlee and Miles, were to follow.[18]

Col. Hugh Mercer was an eminent British soldier, born in Scotland, and educated at the University of Aberdeen. He studied medicine, and afterwards became Assistant Surgeon in the army of Prince Charles Edward, in 1745. He emigrated to America in 1747, and was in Braddock's defeat of 1755, was severely wounded, and wandering alone through the wilderness, reached Fort Cumberland. In 1758, he became Lieutenant Colonel, and marched under General Forbes to Fort Du Quesne, occupied Fort Ligonier a short time, and was brought to Du Quesne, where he remained in command after

General Forbes left for Philadelphia. At the close of the British and French war he returned to practice as a physician, settling in Fredericksburg, Virginia. While there he drilled the Virginia militia. His subsequent career in the Revolutionary War was one of great brilliancy. Finally, in the attack on Trenton, which he recommended to Washington, refusing quarter, he fell under many bayonet wounds. His funeral at Philadelphia was attended, so it was said, by 30,000 persons, It is possible, that being found fighting a second time, under a flag of rebellion, he might have thought that capture meant death or long imprisonment, and therefore he preferred death with honor.

The depletion of Fort Pitt, just mentioned, caused General Monkton to ask of the Pennsylvania Assembly more troops to garrison Fort Pitt and Forts Augusta and Allen,[19] during the winter.

For this purpose he addressed Governor James Hamilton by letter, dated August 21st, 1760. The Governor submitted the letter to the Assembly, with his recommendation to comply with the request. On the 12th September, 1760, the Assembly answered the Governor, stating that they would adjourn in a few days, and that it would take more time than could be spared to determine how far it would be reasonable to impose on their constituents, the burden of garrisoning these fortifications, in view of the many taxes already imposed.

Hearing of the result through Mr. Peters,[20] General Monckton again addressed Governor Hamilton, repeating his request and asking it to be laid before the new Assembly. His letter was dated at Fort Pitt, September 2, 1760. On the 15th October, 1760, the Governor laid the matter before the House. On the 17th October, the Assembly answered, stating the favorable change in military operations; Canada having been reduced, and her subjects having taken the oath of allegiance and fidelity; stating also other reasons, the request to supply the troops was therefore refused. Thus the General was left to do the best he could; without additional troops for garrison duty. However, the subject did not rest there. General Amherst, believing more troops necessary, wrote from New York, February 27th, 1761, to Governor Hamilton, that the Forts and Posts within the communication to Pittsburgh must be kept up, for the protection and security of the country; and therefore requested, that on the receipt of his letter, he would call the Assembly together to raise forthwith three hundred men, properly officered for the service, and when raised, cause the levies immediately to be set in motion to the Forts and Posts, agreeably to the proportions which General Monckton might allot to each. Accordingly, the Governor convened the Assembly, who passed a bill to raise three hundred troops to relieve the Forts and Posts communicating with Pittsburgh.

On the 17th of March, 1761, Governor Hamilton issued his proclamation for the enlistment of the men. A bounty of six pounds was offered as a free gift to each person enlisting, and nine pounds advance money, including clothing. Each officer was to receive twenty shillings for every able-bodied man he should enlist, after he had passed muster at the town of Carlisle.

On the 15th March, 1761, General Amherst sent to Governor Hamilton a letter from William Pitt, the British Minister, dated White-hall, December 17th, 1760, stating that the "Falmouth," in which the original was sent, had been captured by the enemy, and triplicates of it had just arrived in the sloop Tamur. He urged with great force the necessity of complying with his Majesty's orders.

Mr. Pitt, in this long letter, stated that his Majesty had at heart the vigorous prosecution of the war to compel a peace, and the necessity of employing the regular forces in this work, and requesting the Governor to use his utmost endeavors, with all proper dispatch, to raise men; and to hold themselves in readiness to march to such places as his Majesty's Commander-in-Chief should appoint; and enjoining on him to have nothing in view but the good of the King's service, and a due subordination of the whole to his Majesty's Commander. The letter contains various injunctions relative to the troops and the service. While couched in courteous phrase, the tone of the letter was peremptory.

General Amherst wrote again March 2d, 1761, regretting that the Assembly had adjourned before receiving the King's orders, and informing the Governor that General Monckton would be on his way to Philadelphia to station the three hundred men voted by the Assembly.

Western Pennsylvania in the Seven Years' War 1754 - 1763

PENNSYLVANIA

Blue Mountain

Laurel Hill

Allegheny River

W. Branch Susquehannah

Ohio River

Monongahela River

Susquehannah River

Fort Presqu'Ile

Fort Riviere aux Boeufs

Fort Machault

Kuskuskees

Sawkunk

Logstown

Seneca Town

Kittanning

Fort Duquesne

Battle of Monongahela
July 9, 1755

Fort Ligonier

Fort Necessity

Fort Cumberland

Fort Bedford

Standing Stone

Fort Granville

Fort Shirley

Fort Augusta

Harris's Ferry

Carlisle

Shippensburg

Lancaster

General Robert Monckton was an English soldier, born in England, and a son of the first Viscount of Galway. His military career began in Flanders, in 1742; and he became Lieutenant Colonel of the 47th Regiment. In 1753, beginning in America, at Halifax, he was in quite active service in the north, and became Governor of Nova Scotia in 1756. In 1757, he was transferred to the 60th, or Royal American Regiment. While in service in the north, he commanded part of the forces which captured Acadia, and expelled its innocent inhabitants from their homes, confiscating their property, pursuing them as fugitives, and deporting them from the Island. The conduct of Great Britain in this affair was unworthy of her fair fame. He became Brigadier-General in 1758, and was present and wounded severely at the capture of Quebec. He was in command at Fort Pitt, as we have seen, in 1760. He rose to the rank of Major-General, and was eminent in his subsequent career. He was offered a commission in the war against the Colonies, but greatly to his credit, refused to fight against them.

Governor Hamilton convened the Assembly, and on the 3d day of April, 1761, sent his message to them, with Mr. Pitt's letter, urging compliance with his Majesty's orders. On the 10th of April, the Assembly sent their answer.

After stating their zeal and loyalty, and desire to comply with the requisitions laid upon them, they say:

> But upon taking a view of the present circumstances of the Province; the load of debt already imposed upon the people; the mode pointed out to us for granting supplies, contrary to those rights which we hold ourselves indispensably bound to preserve; the injury which must attend the property of our constituents, should we pursue that mode, and the great insecurity of our bills of credit, should we deviate from it, we are of opinion it is not in our power to grant the aid required, consistent with that justice and duty we owe to the people we represent.

They then proceeded to state what had already been done by the Assembly, the sums granted, the laws passed, the many difficulties encountered, the taxation of the estates of the Penns, the mischief and confusion brought upon the Province, and other reasons, contained in a long response, signed by Isaac Norris, the Speaker.[21]

On the 10th of April, General Amherst, having heard through a private source of the probable refusal of the Assembly, wrote to Governor Hamilton:

> I cannot therefore refrain from expressing my highest disapprobation of so unwarrantable a non-compliance with the King's requisition, which if they will not reconsider and act up to, (as I am inclined to think and to hope they will,) I must represent their backwardness to his Majesty, whose displeasure, I should think they would be sorry to incur, and yet how can they expect to avoid it, if they persist obstinately in the rejection of his demands, the result of which may be no less than of the worst consequences to the operations, that must accordingly lie at their door, and which they will regret when it is too late.

The remainder of the letter was in the same vein, and proves that his Majesty's high officers were not less peremptory than himself. As a soldier, General Amherst knew how to dragoon others.

This letter was submitted by the Governor to the Assembly in a very spicy message. The result was the passage of a bill granting 30,000 pounds to the King, which was objected to by the Governor, on account of certain obnoxious provisions. Another controversy followed, but as the matters in dispute do not pertain strictly to Fort Pitt, they will not be pursued. Enough has been given to exhibit the great trials through which the Province passed during the war with France, begun at Fort Pitt. It is the old story of a contest between power and weakness, in the pursuit of the Sovereign's own purposes. It is evident, however, that the spirit of liberty was arising, soon to appear in resistance, followed by war.

Fort Pitt was destined to undergo further trials. The western Indians, who had been under the influence of France, continued hostile and active, notwithstanding the treaty of peace between Great Britain and France in 1763, by which France ceded to Great Britain, all her posessions in America east of the Mississippi river, except the Isle of Orleans. Fort Pitt, Fort Ligonier, Fort Bedford, and other forts were kept in constant alarm. Fort Pitt was beleaguered, and in such danger, it became necessary to send forces to relieve it, and this led to the expedition of Col. Henry Bouquet, in 1763, with an army of 500 men by the Pennsylvania route, through Bedford and Ligonier. It may be observed, by the way, that Fort Ligonier was named after Sir John Ligonier, Commander-in-Chief of the land forces of Great Britain, who afterwards rose to the title of an English Earl.[22]

General Amherst informed the Governor, June 12th, 1763, that by advices from Col. Bouquet, then at Carlisle, intelligence had reach him of the bad intentions of the Indians, and the necessity of sending troops. In a second letter of the 25th, he says it appears from intelligence from all quarters, that the Indians are determined to push their depredations, and no time should be lost in calling the Assembly together, and pressing them to raise troops.

On the 6th of July, 1763, the Assembly having met, the Governor laid before the House a letter of Col. Bouquet, then at Carlisle, as follows:

> I am sorry to inform you, that our forts at Presque Isle; Le Boeuff, and Venango, are cut off, and the garrisons massacred by the savages, except one officer and seven men, who have escaped from Le Boeuff.[23] Fort Pitt was briskly attacked on the 22d, (June,) but only a few men killed and wounded, and dispersed the enemy. Fort Ligonier has likewise stood a vigorous attack by means of some men who reinforced that small garrison from the militia, at Bedford. The Indians expect strong reinforcements to make new attempts on these forts. If the measures I had the honor to recommend to you in my letter of yesterday, are not immediately put into execution, I forsee the ruin of the part of the Province this side of the Susquehanna; and as York county would be covered by Cumberland, I think they ought to join in assisting to build some forts, and saving the harvests. It would not be less necessary to send immediately arms and ammunition to be distributed to the inhabitants to defend the reapers.

In consequence of these representations, the Assembly passed two bills, which were signed by the Governor on the 8th of July, 1763, one an Act for regulating the hire of carriages employed in his Majesty's service; the other for regulating the officers and soldiers in the pay of the Province.

Col. Bouquet soon marched westward from Carlisle, then the central encampment of the troops. When he reached Bushy Run, in Westmoreland county, about twenty miles from the Post, he was ambushed by the Indians, who had learned of his march, and left the siege of Fort Pitt to meet him. Then ensued a most sanguinary and protracted battle, lasting two days, in which the Indians had almost prevailed, until Bouquet, by an ingenious and successful manœuvre, fell upon the Indians in flank and rear and utterly routed them. The losses of the troops were excessively severe, (about 50 killed and 60 wounded,) scarcely compensated by the loss of the Indians, (about 40 killed, including some of their chiefs.) The army reached Fort Pitt in August, 1763, and relieved it, finding it in a great strait. The Indians had surrounded and so closely watched it, all communication with the fort had been cut off.[24]

From Fort Pitt, in October, 1764, Col. Bouquet marched against the western Indians; building a fort on the Tuscarawas, and compelling them to sue for peace.[25]

Col. Henry Bouquet was an eminent soldier, both in Europe and America. He was a Swiss, born at Rolle, Switzerland. After he came to America he became Lieutenant-Colonel of a regiment of Swiss and Germans raised here. A writer says:

He was of majestic stature, of great genius, and under a cold and imposing appearance possessed a sensitive heart. Firmness, intrepidity and presence of mind in the greatest dangers, virtues so essential to a commander, were natural to him. His presence inspired confidence and commanded respect; it encouraged his soldiers, it confounded his enemies.

The same writer says:

Immediately after the peace was concluded with the Indians, the King made him Brigadier-General and Commander of the troops in all the southern colonies of British America. He died at

Pensacola, (in 1767,) lamented by his friends, and regretted universally.

When at Fort Pitt, Bouquet erected a redoubt, in which he placed a stone inscribed, "Col. Bouquet, A. D. 1764." The writer has often seen it in the front wall of the building. It was removed by the city of Pittsburgh to a place of safety to preserve it.[26]

Comparative peace prevailed after Col. Boquet's expedition into the Indian country. But a new cause of alarm began to show itself in the illegal settlement of the Redstone region, on, the Monongahela. The Indians complained of this as a trespass on their lands. It became a subject of correspondence between General Gage, the Commander-in-Chief of the British forces in America, and, Governor Penn.[27] In his letter of December 7th, 1767, General Gage made a strong appeal to the Governor. He feared the dissatisfaction of the Indians would lead to a rupture, and another Indian war. This led to long consideration by the Assembly, and report of a bill to remove the settlers and prevent settlements on lands of the Indians not yet purchased.

Among the grievances of the Indians was the unprovoked murder of a number while traveling through their own lands. These disturbances led to the treaty of the Penns with the Six Nations, at Fort Stanwix, November 5th, 1768. The boundary in the western part of the State was agreed by it to be run from, Kittanning down the Ohio, (Allegheny,) to the western boundary of the Province; thence along the western boundary to the southern boundary; and thence along the southern boundary to the east side of the Allegheny mountains. This included the Indian title to all the lands east of the Allegheny river, and west of the mountains, permitting, thereafter, the settlement of the Redstone region.

After this treaty the events were so unimportant, it is unnecessary to relate them, until the abandonment of Fort Pitt by the order of General Gage, and the possession of it seized upon by the order of Governor Dunmore, under claim of title on the part of Virginia.

In the month of October, 1772, Major Edmundson, then commanding the Fort, received the order of General Gage to abandon

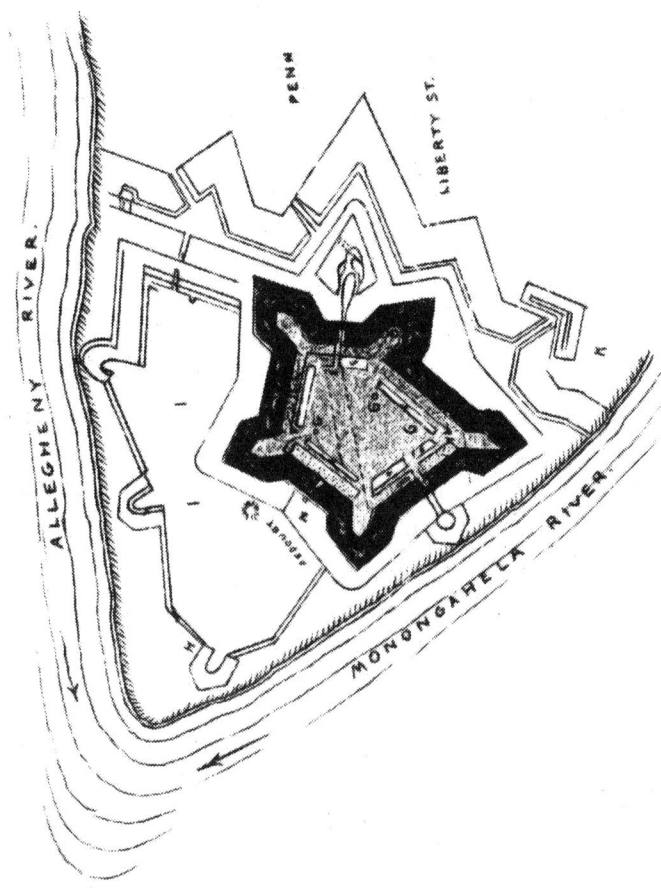

Plan of Fort Pitt in 1761.
From George Dallas Alberts, *Frontier Forts of Western Pennsylvania*, Vol. II, 1916.

A – BARRACKS, ALREADY BUILT. B – COMMANDANTS HOUSE, NOT BUILT.
C – STORE HOUSE. D – POWDER MAGAZINES. E – CASEMENT COMPLETE.
F – STORE HOUSE FOR FLOUR ETC. G – WELLS IN TWO OF WHICH ARE PUMPS.
H – FORT DUQUESNE. I.I. HORN WORK TO COVER FRENCH BARRACKS.
K FIRST FORT PITT DESTROYED. N. SALLY PORT.

Fort Pitt.[28] In consequence of this order the property at the Fort was sold at a great sacrifice. The Fort was then evacuated, leaving only three men to take care of the boats and batteaux kept for the purpose of maintaining the communication down the Ohio. The evacuation created great consternation among the people, who feared Indian hostilities might again visit them. This caused measures to be taken to induce General Gage to recall his order, and again occupy the fort.

In reply to a letter of Governor Penn,[29] of August 29th, 1772, urging the recall, General Gage answered from New York November 2d, stating it was too late to send counter orders to Fort Pitt. He added that he thought the abandonment of little consequence. It was no asylum for settlers, and could not cover the frontiers. It was of no use except for military deposits.

General Thomas Gage was a British soldier, born in Sussex. He was Major of the 44th Regiment in 1747, and was in Braddock's expedition against Du Quesne, then ranking as Lieutenant-Colonel. He participated in the battle of July 9th, 1755, and though wounded, rallied the troops to aid in carrying the wounded Braddock to a place of safety. In 1758, he was with General Abercrombie in his disastrous expedition against Ticonderoga. In August, 1759, he was in command of the Department of Ontario, as a Brigadier-General; participated in the conquest of Canada in 1759, and was appointed Military Governor at Montreal. In December, 1763, he succeeded General Amherst as Commander-in-Chief in America, and directed the affairs of the army until February, 1773, when he returned to England. It is unnecessary to follow his career further, except to say it was of great importance, being in command at Boston in 1774–75, and taking part against the Colonists in the primary movements of the Revolutionary War.

A most serious consequence of the abandonment of Fort Pitt was the taking possession of the fort by Governor Dunmore, through Dr. Connolly, his agent and lieutenant, for the purpose, of asserting the claim of Virginia to the territory at the head of the Ohio. By the Charter of Charles the Second to William Penn, granting to him the Province of Pennsylvania, the river Delaware was made the eastern boundary of the grant, and the Charter then proceeded: "The said lands to extend westward five degrees in longitude, to be computed from the said eastern bounds." The Delaware being a crooked line, the question arose, from what part of it the five degrees of longitude should be measured? At that early day the longitude of Fort Pitt, as well as its true distance from the Delaware was unknown. Indeed, there were no instruments at Pittsburgh to ascertain latitude arid longitude. Virginia claimed that the head of Ohio was outside of the limits of Pennsylvania, and within the territory of Virginia, whose Charter admitted of a latitude, in the west, capable of almost any enlargement. George Croghan, in a letter to David Semple, April 4th, 1774, said he had long been convinced that Fort Pitt and its dependencies were without the limits of Pennsylvania. On the other hand, others asserted that Pittsburgh was six miles within the Pennsylvania boundary. Lord Dunmore was determined to assert the title of Virginia, and for this purpose sent out Dr. Connolly to take possession of Fort Pitt and make some repairs. He did so, and named the Fort "Dunmore."

He was afterwards commissioned with civil as well as military authority. Great disturbances ensued, the civil officers of Pennsylvania being arrested and imprisoned by Connolly, who even took possession of the Court at Hannastown. A frightful state of affairs existed in all the region around Pittsburgh.

It is not the design of this sketch to enter into the general history of affairs outside of the immediate relations of Fort Pitt. The claim of Virginia and occurrences arising out of it, will therefore not be pursued further. The course of Lord Dunmore and his agents in the west, led to the war with the Indians in 1774, known as "Dunmore's War."

After a time the Fort regained its name "Fort Pitt," and was occupied under the Continental Congress as the headquarters of the Western Military Department, by Generals Hand, McIntosh, Brodhead and Irvine. By this time a village had arisen near the Fort, which led to a survey of the manor of Pittsburgh by the Penns, followed by a survey of the plat of Pittsburgh, under the Penns, in 1784, including the ground occupied by the Fort. The survey was made by Col. George Woods, of Bedford, aided by his son John Woods and Thomas Vickroy.[30]

The events during the occupancy of Fort Pitt under the Congress, are briefly told by the writer in his sketch of "Fort McIntosh and its Times," to which reference may be had.

Notes:

[1] William Pitt (1708–1778) served as secretary of war, 1757–1761 and was responsible for overseeing the conduct of the war. Major General Jeffery Amherst (1717–1797) served as commander-in-chief of British forces in North America 1758–1763. William Denny (1709–1765) was governor of Pennsylvania from 1756–1759.

[2] Brigadier General John Stanwix (1690–1765) had served in the army since 1706. He was appointed colonel of the 1st battalion, 62nd Regiment of Foot (later the 60th) on January 1 1756. He had commanded in Pennsylvania in 1756–1757 and was promoted to brigadier general on December 27, 1757. He again commanded in Pennsylvania from March 18 1759 to May 4 1760.

[3] Colonel Hugh Mercer (1725–1777), a doctor by trade, has served as a surgeon in the Jacobite Rebellion of 1745. He fled to America in 1747 and was lieutenant colonel of the 3rd Battalion, Pennsylvania Regiment in 1758. He commanded Fort Pitt from December 1758 until the arrival of Stanwix in August, 1759. He was serving as a brigadier general in the Continental Army when was killed near Princeton, NJ on January 12, 1777.

[4] Fort Bedford, at Raystown (now Bedford, PA), at the crossing of the Juniata River, was built by Bouquet in June 1758 as a depot for the advance on Fort Duquesne. It was occupied by British soldiers until the early 1770s. The Bedford County militia maintained a garrison there during the War of American Independence and local settlers used the remains as a place of defense through the 1780s. See www.motherbedford.com.

[5] Sir William Johnson (1715–1774) was superintendent for Indian affairs in the northern department.

[6] Captains Thomas Waggener (d. circa 1760) and Henry Woodward (circa 1730–1790) were both captains in the Virginia Regiment. Captains John Prentice, Asher Clayton, Thomas Smallman, and Edward Ward were all serving in the Pennsylvania Regiment. All were stationed in the garrison at Fort Pitt in 1759. Edward Ward was the same officer who had surrendered the site of Fort Duquesne to Contrecoeur in 1754. Listings of the officers serving in the Pennsylvania Regiment during the Seven Years' War can be found in John B. Linn and William H. Egle, *Pennsylvania Provincial Archives, Second Series,* Harrisburg, PA: B. F. Meyers, 1876.

[7] This would most likely be Lieutenants Edmond Matthews, Martin Heidler, Edward Biddle (1738–1779), Nicholas Conrad, John Kennedy, Robert Anderson, and Thomas Hutchins (1730–1789) of the Pennsylvania Regiment. Lieutenants Jethro Sumner (circa 1733–1785) and William Dangerfield (d. 1781) were serving in the Virginia Regiment. Lieutenant John Wright was serving in the Lower County companies and was promoted to captain on May 2, 1759. See John B. Linn and William H. Egle, *Pennsylvania Provincial Archives, Second Series,* Harrisburg, PA: B. F. Meyers, 1876, 2:581.

[8] These are probably Ensigns Hugh Crawford (d. 1770), Robert Crawford, and Jacob Morgan, Jr., all serving in the Pennsylvania Regiment.

[9] John Ormsby (1720–1805) served as commissary under Forbes and became an early resident of Pittsburgh. Mr. Aden is possibly George Allen, who along with Samuel Lightfoot and James Kenny opened a storehouse in Pittsburgh in 1759. Samuel Lightfoot died on July 30, 1759. See John W. Jordan, Ed., "The Journal of James Kenny," *Pennsylvania Magazine of History and Biography,* Vol. 37.

[10] This would actually be Captain William Trent (1715–1757) long a fur trader in the Ohio Valley, and Thomas McKee (circa 1695–1769) father of Alexander McKee.

[11] George Croghan noted in his journal that he clothed 375 warriors at the conference. There was probably an even greater number present as that number was only those warriors "that had not been Cloathed before." King Beaver, or Tamaqua (d. 1769), the Delaware chief of Kuskuskee was the principal speaker for the Native Americans. For Croghan's brief account of the proceedings see Wainwright, Nicholas B., ed., "George Croghan's Journal 1759–1763," *The Pennsylvania Magazine of History and Biography,* Volume 71, No. 4, October 1947, pp. 324–25.

[12] The French force, under the command of François-Marie Le Marchand de Lignery (1703–1759) was gathered at Fort Machault, or Venango, (present-day Franklin, PA). On July 13 they received word of that Fort Niagara was under siege by the British. Lignery departed with all hands on July 14, 1759 to relieve the siege. Forts Machault and Rivière-aux-boeufs were both burned during the withdrawal. Lignery was mortally wounded and his force was defeated outside Fort Niagara at the Battle of La Famille, July 24, 1759. Walter O'Meara, *Guns at the Forks,* Englewood Cliffs, NJ: Prentice-Hall, Inc., 1965, p. 216. For Lignery see C. J. Russ "François-Marie le Marchand de Lignery," in *Dictionary of Canadian Biography,* 3:378–79. For the Battle of La Famille, see Stephen Brumwell, *Redcoats: The British Soldier and War in the Americas 1755–1763,* New York: Cambridge University Press, 2001, pp. 252–254.

[13] Fort Ligonier, at Loyalhannon (present-day Ligonier, PA) was constructed by Bouquet in 1758 during the march on Fort Duquesne. It was garrisoned by British troops until March, 1766.

[14] Captain Harry Gordon (d. 1787), engineer, arrived at forks on August 1 and began construction of the new Fort Pitt on September 3. See O'Meara, p. 218.

[15] It is highly doubtful that Elizabeth Couc Montour, (circa 1667–1752) was the daughter of Count Frontenac. Her parents were more likely Louis Couc Montour and an Algonquian woman named Mitewamegwakwe. She had long served as an interpreter, first in New York, and then in Pennsylvania. Her son Andrew Montour (d. circa 1775) also often served as an interpreter in Pennsylvania. For Madame Montour see Mary Lou Lustig "Madame Montour," in American National Biography On-line at www.anb.org.

[16] Major John Tulleken of the 1st Battalion, 60th Regiment of Foot. He had been commissioned major on April 25, 1757.

[17] Brigadier General Robert Monckton (d. 1782) had served in Nova Scotia and commanded the expedition against Fort Beauséjour in 1755, He served at Louisbourg in 1758 and at Quebec in 1759. He later commanded the expedition against Martinique in 1762.

[18] Captains Edward Biddle (1738–1779), William Clapham, Jr., Robert Anderson, Samuel J. Atlee (1739–1786), and Samuel Miles, all of the Pennsylvania Regiment. Captain John McNeill of the Virginia Regiment marched with Bouquet to Presqu'Île.

[19] Fort Allen was built in January 1756 at present-day Weissport, PA by Pennsylvania militia under the command of Benjamin Franklin. It was garrisoned by Pennsylvania troops until 1761. Fort Augusta, at Sunbury, PA, was built in July 1756 and was garrisoned until 1765.

[20] Richard Peters (1704–1776) was provincial secretary of Pennsylvania.

[21] Isaac Norris (1701–1766) served as speaker of the Pennsylvania Assembly 1750–1766. He is credited with selecting the text from *Leviticus* 25:10 that is inscribed on the Liberty Bell, "Proclaim liberty throughout the land, and to all the inhabitants thereof."

[22] Sir John Ligonier (1680–1770) became captain-general of the British Army on June 29, 1757. He became Earl Ligonier of Ripley on September 10, 1766.

[23] Forts le Beouf and Venango were attacked on June 18, 1763. Fort Presqu'Île was attacked on June 19 and was taken by a force of about 250 warriors on June 20. The first survivors from Fort le Boeuf arrived at Fort Pitt with the news on June 25. See Niles Anderson, *The Battle of Bushy Run,* Harrisburg, PA: Pennsylvania Historical and Museum Commission, 1991, p. 3

[24] The Battle of Bushy Run was fought over two days on August 4–5, 1763. The site is now a park near Harrison City, PA. See Anderson, *Bushy Run.*

[25] Bouquet marched from Fort Pitt on October 4, 1764 and arrived at King Beaver's town at present-day Bolivar, OH on the Tuscarawas River on October 13. Bouquet's fortified storehouse was built at present-day Coshocton, OH. Bouquet met with representatives of the Delaware and Shawnee on October 20.

[26] Bouquet's Redoubt is at Point State Park in Pittsburgh.

[27] John Penn (1729–1795) acted as governor of Pennsylvania 1763–1771 and 1773–1776. He was one of the proprietors.

[28] Major Charles Edmondstone of the 38th Regiment was commander of Fort Pitt at this time.

[29] Richard Penn (1735–1811), younger brother of John, served as governor from 1771–1773. He traveled to England in 1775 in a last-ditch effort to maintain the peace. He remained in England the rest of his life, serving some years in Parliament.

[30] George Woods (d. 1795) had settled at Bedford in 1765. He later served on the Supreme Executive Council of Pennsylvania, 1777–1779. His son John Woods died in 1817. Thomas Vickroy was their assistant.

"LOGSTOWN,"

ON THE OHIO.

WITH

A HISTORICAL SKETCH

By DANIEL AGNEW, LL. D.

Originally Published:

Pittsburgh:
Myers, Shinkle & Co. Printers, Stationers, Binders
1894.

"Logstown,"
on the Ohio

THE RAVAGES of time are fast leveling the landmarks of Indian occupancy in Western Pennsylvania and on the river Ohio. Places where many gathered, and early councils of the red men were held, where affairs of vast importance were transacted, are now unknown, and not a vestige remains to mark the spots then filled with life and activity.

Such has been the fate of Logstown, on the Ohio. In the middle of the last century it was a busy centre of Indian life, where a great trade was carried on with them by the French and the English. Then, too, the Indian nations claimed all the land west of the Allegheny Mountains, and on the Ohio. Not only no vestige marks its once busy scene, but error has transferred its site to the opposite side of the Ohio. The evidence of its true locality is, however, full and absolute to those who choose to delve into the remains of the past; of this hereafter. For the present it is sufficient to say, that Logstown stood on the land, now the property of the Harmony Society, at Economy, a short distance below the town, and on the right or north bank of the Ohio.

In the early settlement of the French on the river St. Lawrence, their progress was northward and westward, leading them to the upper Lakes and to the Mississippi. Their southward war expeditions were toward the British Colonies on the Atlantic. It was not until the middle of the last century they reached Presque Isle, on Lake Erie, and extended eastward to the Allegheny river, by them called the Ohio. They built forts at Presque Isle, Le Boueff on French Creek, and Venango at its junction with the Allegheny. Intending to mark their claim of title to the countries bounding on the Allegheny and Ohio, founded on the alleged discovery of the main Ohio by the Sieur La Salle, about seventy or eighty years before, the Marquis Gallesonier, the French Governor of New France, sent Mons. Celeron down the

Allegheny and Ohio, in the year 1749, to plant the evidence of possession and title along their shores. This he did by burying many inscribed leaden plates at the mouths of their principal tributaries. A translation of one of these may be seen in "Fort McIntosh, and its Times," page 22. This plate was found at the mouth of French Creek, called Toradakoin by the Indians.

A short time before, most probably in 1747, the French had built New Logstown for the Indians inhabiting Western Pennsylvania and the Ohio. It was built on the second rise, or plateau below the town of Economy, in Beaver County. The houses, about thirty, were substantial log cabins, some with stone chimneys. It was here a large trade was carried on between the French and English traders and the Indians. The original town was an Indian village, on the river bottom below the new town, one of the many Indian settlements on the river and creek bottoms of the larger branches. They selected the rich sandy river and creek flats for the cultivation of maize, (Indian corn,) such being level and more easily cultivated in their primitive modes.

The precise time of building the new town is not accurately known, but all the information gathered would fix the date as 1747.[*][1] At this time neither Fort Du Quesne nor Fort Pitt existed, the former being built in 1754, and the latter in 1759. The junction of the rivers Monongahela and Allegheny was then wild and uninhabited. Logstown was therefore the centre of French and Indian affairs.

The first distinct knowledge of Logstown is found in the journal of Conrad Weiser, who was sent by the Pennsylvania Colonial Council to visit the Indians on the Ohio. Conrad Weiser was a German, born in 1696; came with his father, when ten years old, to America; and settled at Schohaire, New York. When a boy he went to live with the chief of the Mohawk nation, to acquire a knowledge of the language, which he mastered, and thus became an efficient interpreter. In 1729, he came to Pennsylvania, and settled in the Tulpehocken valley, near the present town of Womelsdorff. He was employed by

---

[*] Note.—1747 the time supposed when *new* Logstown was built is too early. Referring to the time when the French reached Presque Isle, it is more probable it was not built until after 1754. Post however saw it in 1758.

the Colonial Government in many services; was a justice of the peace, and was commissioned Colonel in a regiment of volunteers in Berks county. He was highly esteemed for his intelligence, honesty, and great reliability, and participated in various matters of great importance. His knowledge of the Indian tongues carried him on missions to the Indians among the Six Nations in New York, and to those westward on the Ohio. A man of great shrewdness, caution and discretion, he was intimately acquainted with the Indian character, and was much respected by them. His residence was in Heidelberg Township, Berks County, where he lived many years, and died in July, 1760.

The Colonial Council being apprised of the efforts of the French to win over the Ohio Indians, felt it proper to take steps to prevent it. Conrad Weiser was called upon to advise with the Council. He took with him, and presented to them, Andrew Montour, a very competent interpreter. The Council sent them to the Ohio, giving Weiser written instructions covering many points of inquiry and discussion. The instructions began by saying:

> This Government having promised the Indians who came from the Ohio in November last, to send you to them early in the spring, and having provided a present of considerable value, you are to proceed thither with all convenient dispatch. Mr. George Croghan, the Indian trader, who is well acquainted with the Indian country, and the best roads to Ohio, has undertaken the convoy of you and the goods, with his own men and horses, at the public expense.

The instructions are too numerous and minute to be recited. They included many points to be learned, such as a perfect knowledge of the number, situation and strength of all the Indians on the Ohio, their temper, and the influence of the tribes. These instructions display great confidence and trust in Weiser's intelligence, discretion and integrity. They are signed by Anthony Palmer, the President of the Council,[2] and dated June 23d, 1748. Weiser kept a full journal of his journey, and of his conferences with the Indians.

He set out from Heidelberg August 11th, 1748, going by the Tuscarowa path, passing Standing Stone, (Huntington), on the Juniata and Frankstown, crossing the "Allegheny Hills," going through the "Clearfields," reaching the "Kiskeminitoes" on the 20th day of August, and on the same day crossing to the Ohio, (Allegheny,) where he took passage by water to Logstown. On the 27th of August, he dined in a Seneca town, where an old Seneca woman reigned, he says, with great authority, and arrived at Logstown that evening, and saluted the town.[3] The Indians returned the salute with about one hundred guns. Great joy appeared in their countenances.

Some of his party went from Logstown up to Koskosky, a large Indian town thirty miles off. Kuskuskee, as it is oftener written, lay on the west side of the Big Beaver, just below the mouth of the Mahoning. Weiser himself went to Beaver Creek, eight miles below, to have some Wampum woven. The journal is very voluminous, containing the preparations made to meet the Indians of various tribes in council, at Logstown, among them naming the "Wandots," Senecas and Delawares. In compliance with his instructions, he states the number of the fighting men of each nation settled on the Ohio, as given by the deputies in council, viz: Senecas, 163; Shawanese, 162; Owandots, 100; Tisagechroamis, 40; Mohawks, 74; Mohicans, 15; Onondagos, 35; Cayugas, 20; Oneidas, 15; Delawares, 165; in all, 789. The count was by bundles of small sticks.[4]

On the 3d of September, he says:

> We set up the Union flag on a long pole; treated all the company with a dram of rum. The King's health was drunk by the Indians and white men. Towards night a great many Indians arrived to attend the Council. There was much firing on both sides. The strangers first saluted the town at a quarter of a mile distance, and at their entry the town's people returned the fire, and also the English traders, of whom there were about twenty.

Being informed that the "Wandots" were going over to the French, and trying to take the Delawares with them, he sent Montour up to the Delaware towns on Beaver Creek, to inquire into the matter, and was informed they had no correspondence with the Wandots that way.

In this Council with the Wandots, they informed him that they came from the French on account of hard usage; that the French got their young men to go to war against their enemies, and would use them like slaves; and their goods were so dear, the Indians could not buy them; that one hundred fighting men came to join the English, and more would follow.

The goods sent out by Croghan were delayed so long, some distrust was evidenced, But finally they arrived, and were divided into five shares for distribution; one to the Senecas, one to the Cayugas, Oneidas, Onondagos and Mohawks, one to the Delawares, another to the Owandots, Tisaghechroamis, and Mohicans, and the last to the Shawanese. The Indians expressed great satisfaction, and were well pleased with the cessation of arms, referring to the peace declared between England and France.

On behalf of the President and Council, Weiser addressed each Nation separately, and received replies from their representative chiefs or deputies. Many of the replies are interesting, but must be omitted.

The effect of Weiser's mission was important in attaching many of the Indians to the English, and preventing others from being carried off to the French.

The next important notice of Logstown is found in a letter from George Croghan to Governor Hamilton, dated at Logstown, December 16th, 1750. He arrived the day before, and found there thirty warriors of the Six Nations, who were going to war against the Catawba Indians. They told him that Joncaire, then a very influential and active agent of the French, was at an Indian town about 150 miles up the river, where he intended to build a fort, if he could get the consent of the Indians. It seems probable the town meant was at the mouth of French Creek, where the French built a fort about that time.[5]

He refers to the design of the Twightwees[6] to settle up the river, and their determination to hold no treaty of peace with the French, and to other matters of importance.

The Assembly of the Province had made provision for a present to the Indians on the Ohio, of goods promised to them by the Council. In consequence of the inability of Conrad Weiser, who was engaged to go to the Six Nations in New York, George Croghan was appointed to go to Logstown, to convey to them the present. Instructions were given to Croghan, dated April 25th, 1751. Of his proceedings he kept a journal, which he afterwards submitted to the Governor, dated at his home, in Pennsylvania, June 10th, 1751. These dates give an approximate time required to make the journey to Logstown and return, and the proceedings there.

Croghan took with him Andrew Montour, the interpreter, and reached Logstown May 18th, 1751. The Indians of a number of tribes attended, and received him favorably. A large council was held.

Croghan states that on the 20th of May, Joncaire, the French agent, came from the head of the Ohio (Allegheny) with forty Indian warriors of the Six Nations, and one Frenchman. On the 21st, a council was called by Joncaire of all the Indians in the town, and he addressed them thus:

> CHILDREN:—I desire you may now give me an answer from your hearts to the speech of Monsieur Shularone (the commander of the party of two hundred Frenchmen that went down the river two years ago) made to you. His speech was, that their father, the Governor of Canada, desired his children on the Ohio to turn away the English traders from amongst them, and to discharge them from ever coming there again, or on any of the branches, on pain of incurring his displeasure; and to enforce that speech he gave a very large belt, of wampum.

Immediately one of the chiefs of the Six Nations got up and made the following speech:

> "FATHERS:—I mean you that call yourselves our fathers, hear what I am going to say to you: You desire we may turn our brothers the English away, and not suffer them to trade with us again. I now tell you from our hearts, we will not, for we ourselves brought them here to live, and they shall live among us as long as there is one of us alive. You are always threatening our brothers what you will do to them, and in particular that man, (pointing to me.) Now, if you have anything to say to our brothers, tell it to him, if you be a man, as you Frenchmen always say you are, and the head of all nations. Our brothers are the people we will trade with, and not you. Go tell your Governor to ask the Onondago council if I don't speak the minds of all the Six Nations," and returned the belt.

On a subsequent day, (May 25th,) Joncaire apologized to Mr. Croghan, saying his orders came from the French Governor, and he was obliged to obey, though he was sensible the Indians would not receive his declaration.

The Indians present came from many places down and up the river, the Big Beaver, and other points.

The method of proceeding by the Indians as to a disposition of their land is interesting, as illustrated by an example related in the journal. A Dunkard, from Virginia, came to Logstown, to request the consent of the Six Nations to his making a settlement on land on the "Yogh-yo-ganie." The Indians answered it was not in their power to dispose of lands; that he must first be recommended by the Governor of Pennsylvania, and then apply to the council at Onondaga.

It will be remembered that the title of the Indians to the whole of Western Pennsylvania was not extinguished at that time. The treaties made at Fort Stanwix had not then been made. See "Fort Pitt and its Times," page 92.

A treaty between Croghan and the Indians was made at Logstown, on the 28th of May, 1751. Deputies from the Six Nations, the Delawares, Shawanese, Awandots and Twightwees were present. Croghan, in behalf of Governor Hamilton made separate speeches to the deputies of each nation.

An indication of the trade at Logstown is found in the names given by Croghan of the English traders present, viz: Thomas Kinton, Samuel Cuggens, Jacob Pyatt, John Owens, Thomas Ward, Joseph Nellson, James Brown, Dennis Sullivan, Paul Pearce, and Caleb Lamb.[7]

An Indian custom at the close of a speech was to signify approval by the cry "Yo-ha." For example, it is stated, "The speaker at the close of his speech handed a belt of wampum, which was received with a Yo-ha." One is tempted to think that the savages at some of our colleges learned their yell from these.

The speeches of Governor Hamilton, by Croghan, in his name, were answered *seriatim* by the Indians, after consultation among themselves.

The journal states the proceeding thus: "A speech received from the Six Nations. The speaker directed his discourse to the Governor of Pennsylvania." The names of the chiefs were then stated, and the name of the speaker. That of the Six Nations was "Toanohiso." The speeches show directness and business shrewdness.[8]

George Croghan, who filled so large a space in the affairs of the west, was an Indian trader. He was by birth an Irishman, educated at Dublin. His residence was at Pennsboro, in Cumberland county, nearly opposite Harris' Ferry, (now Harrisburg.) He was known as an Indian trader on the shores of Lake Erie, as early as 1746. He acquired an ample knowledge of the Indian tongues, and became a man of importance among that people. At one time he was wealthy, but lost nearly all by the ravages of the French Indians. In General Braddock's unfortunate expedition, he was a Captain, and present at the battle of July 9th, 1755, remaining with the general till his death. Afterwards he became an Indian Agent under Sir William Johnson, and was his Deputy in charge of the Ohio Indians. In this capacity he held numerous conferences with the Indians, and was engaged in many missions to them, some as far westward as the Illinois. He was not the ancestor of Mrs. Captain Schenley, whose Allegheny county interests are so well known. William Croghan, the husband of Mary O'Hara, second daughter of General James O'Hara, and the father of Mrs. Schenley, was a son of Major William Croghan, an officer in a Virginia regiment. William Croghan, the son, was a frequent visitor at the office of Henry Baldwin, in Pittsburgh, when the writer was a student of law in that office. This was in the year 1826. He was at that time paying attention to Miss O'Hara.

The next noticeable mention of Logstown is found in the journal of Major George Washington, of his visit to the French forts on French Creek, at Venango, and Le Boueff. He reached Logstown November 25th, 1753. There he waited some days completing his arrangements to go to Venango, and left for that place December 4th, 1753. See an account more at large in "Fort McIntosh, and its Times," page 24. His journal is exceedingly interesting, as all such accounts are, but is too long to abstract. The chief matter to be noticed now, is the importance attached to Logstown, at that time, as a place of trade and population, making it a point to be visited. No fort had then been built at the head of the main Ohio, where Du Quesne was constructed in the next year, (1754.) After that year we hear but little of Logstown, the events of history taking place at Du Quesne and its vicinity.

Washington's defeat in 1754, and surrender at Fort Necessity, and Braddock's defeat at Turtle Creek, in 1755, left the French in possession of the Ohio territory until the abandonment of Fort Du Quesne, on the approach of General John Forbes' army in November, 1758. In the next year, 1759, Fort Pitt was commenced, and finished in 1760.

During the year 1758, and before the advance of General Forbes on Du Quesne, another important journal is found in that of Christian Frederick Post, of his mission to the Ohio Indians, with a message from the Colonial Council of Pennsylvania, to the Delaware, Shawanese and Mingoes settled there. In that journal Logstown again comes into prominent view.[9]

He began his journey July 15th, 1758, going by Fort Allen (on the Lehigh,) and reaching Fort Augusta, (Sunbury,) on the Susquehanna, July 25th. On the 12th of August he came to "Conaquonashon," where, he says, was an old Indian town, fifteen miles from Kuskuskee. On reaching Kuskuskee, he was received hospitably by King Beaver, (of the Turtle tribe of the Delawares,) and found fifteen Frenchmen there building houses for the Indians. Much that is interesting transpired there, but it is too long for notice. On the 20th of August, Post reached Sawkunk, at the mouth of the Big Beaver, and was roughly received. The Indians there were determined to take him to Fort Du Quesne to meet the French and many other Indians there. He opposed this much, but was compelled to go, reaching Logstown on the night of the 23d, where he was received kindly. On the 24th, he came in sight of the Fort, but refused to cross the Allegheny. The Indians at the Fort crossed over to see him. Much ado took place, the French coming over and demanding him of the Indians. They refused however to permit them to take him, saying "they would hear no more about it, but to send them 100 loaves of bread." There was much whispering among the French and Indians; but the latter remained firm.

On the afternoon of the 25th, 300 Canadians arrived at the Fort, and reported more were to follow, with forty battoes loaded with ammunition. Among the Indians were many well known chiefs, for example, Captain Killbuck,[10] afterwards the claimant of Smoky Island, opposite the Pittsburgh point.

Post mentions that many Irish traders endeavored to "spirit" up the Indians against the English.

On the 26th, a council was held by the French with their own Indians, in which it was proposed to cut off all the Delaware chiefs present, and then the Delawares would give them no more trouble. The Tawas[11] answered, "no; we cannot do this thing, for though there is but a handful here, they fire a strong people, spread over a great distance, and whatever they agree to must be."

At a council on the opposite side to the Fort, the French insisted that Post should be delivered up to them. The Indians refused to consent, and next morning Post set off before daylight, reaching Sawkunk, (Beaver,) where he was now well received. On the 28th of August, he set out for Kuskuskee, with a company of over twenty Indians. At that place he dined with Shingiss.[12] Much feasting took place, and consultations among the Indians. Shortly before he left, a council was held, and a very satisfactory answer to the Governor was given to Post.

A thing of much concern to the Indians was the approach of the army under General Forbes, of which they had learned, thinking that they might be cut off. They even feared that the English and French would unite against them. They appealed to Post to tell them the truth, saying: "Now brother, you are here with us, you are our own flesh and blood, speak from the bottom of your heart, will not the French and the English join together to cut off the Indians?" Post declared, with great feeling, that he told them the whole truth, ending by saying, "I do declare before God, that the English never did, nor never will join the French to destroy you." He then explained the relations of the English and French, to convince them. They seemed to be satisfied.

During his stay at Kuskuskee, 200 French and Indians arrived on their way to Fort Du Quesne. The French threatened to catch him privately, and take his scalp.

On the 9th of September Post left, making a most painful and laborious journey homeward, taking unusual paths to avoid being waylaid, and crossing the Susquehanna, (West Branch,) six times, and lying in the woods thirty-two nights, with the heavens his only covering, before reaching Fort Augusta, (Sunbury.) His life was often in danger, but he was saved only by the friendship and honest intentions of the Indians.

In reading this journal one is struck with the true Indian character, exhibiting a sense of right, of honor, proper sentiment, and honest intention, more than it is usual to attribute to them. The Indian is seen by the whites chiefly in a state of war, when his wild nature, heated by his sense of wrongs, displays itself in practices the most savage and inhumane. His anger and revenge drive him on to deeds of the greatest barbarity. But in his own wigwam and native forest, he feels the common sentiments of human nature, and evidences a sense of right and honor, which display him in a very different aspect. Still he is uncultivated and a savage.

General Forbes army arrived at Fort Du Quesne on the 24th of November, 1858,[13] to find it abandoned and in ruin. Fort Pitt was built in the following year and finished in 1760, The Indians then deserted many of their towns, and Logstown was no longer a prominent place of trade and council.

Christian Frederick Post, before General Forbes reached Fort Du Quesne, had made a second journey to the Indians on the Ohio with a message from Governor Denny, of Pennsylvania. He set out on the 25th of October, 1758. This journey, like the former, contains much that is important and interesting, but as only one material reference to Logstown is made, the journal will not be adverted to, except to state what he said as to Logstown. On the 2d of December, 1758, he left Sawkunk, (mouth of Beaver,) for Pittsburgh. He says:

The Beaver creek being very high, it was almost two o'clock in the afternoon before we came over the creek; this land seems to be very rich. I, with my companion, Ketiuskund's son,[14] came to Logstown, situated on a hill. On the east end is a great piece of low land, where the old Logstown used to stand. In the new Logstown, the French have built about thirty houses for the Indians. They have a large corn field on the south side, where the corn stands ungathered.

This cornfield, cultivated on the opposite or south side from Logstown, evidently explains the origin of the belief of the early settlers of Beaver county, that Logstown stood on the south side of the Ohio.

The only further notice of Logstown worth stating is found in the journal of Major George Washington, (from October 5th to December 1st, 1770,) of his tour down the Ohio to view lands to be apportioned among the officers and soldiers of the French war.

On the 20th of October, he encamped with Col. Croghan and Lieut. Hamilton,[15] about four miles above Logstown. On the 21st, leaving the encampment, where he parted with Croghan and the company, he reached Logstown and breakfasted there, and at eleven o'clock reached the mouth of Beaver. No Indians are mentioned, and as this was in 1770, six years after Col. Bouquet's march, when he found Logstown deserted, the occupants were certainly whites.

It remains only to furnish the conclusive evidence of the true site of Logstown. It is proved by early maps and documents corresponding to the statement of Post in his second journal.

A map of the British and French Dominions in North America, particularly showing (it says) the French encroachments through all the British plantations, from Nova Scotia down to the Gulf of Mexico. On the, face of the map is a narrative of these encroachments, filling quite a large space. The map has no date, but contains internal evidence it was made not later than 1753. Fort Du Quesne (erected in 1754) is not marked upon it. Logstown is found marked in its proper relative position, on the north side of the Ohio. This agrees with the journals of Conrad Weiser, Post and Croghan, and the facts already mentioned.

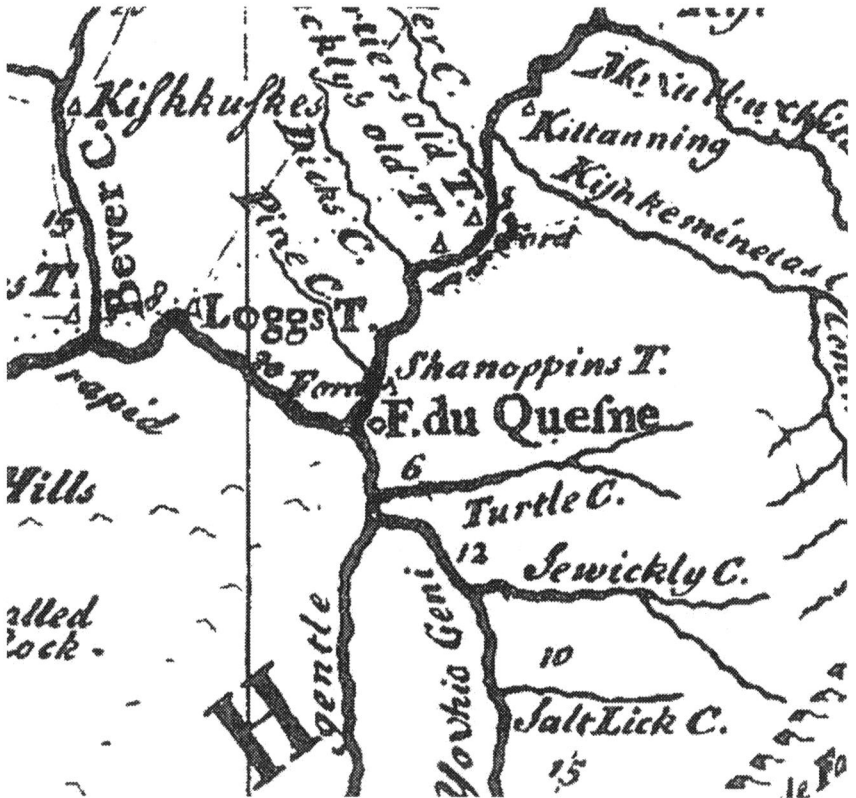

Detail from Lewis Evans, *A General Map of the Middle British Colonies in North America,* Philadelphia, 1755, showing the location of Logstown in comparison to Fort Duquesne.

   2.   A map made by Lewis Evans[16] in 1755, of the middle British Colonies and Indian Nations adjacent, viz :

Virginia, Maryland, Delaware, Pennsylvania, New York, Connecticut and Rhode Island,—Of Acquanishuonigy, the country of the Confederate Indians,—Comprehending Aquanishuonigy proper, their place of residence,—Ohio and Tiiuxsoxruntie, their deer hunting countries, Couxsaxrage, and Skaniadarade, their Beaver hunting countries,—Of Lakes Erie, Ontario and Champlain,—And part of New France.

"Wherein is also shown the ancient and present seats of the Indian Nations."

Tables of distances and valuable notes are given on the face. It was published under an Act of Parliament. Logstown occupies its proper place on the north side of the Ohio, and Fort Du Quesne is laid down upon it.

3. A map found in a most interesting volume, the work of Captain Knox, a British soldier in command in America, in the years 1757, 1758, 1759, 1760, adds another proof to the chain. It was published by him in London, in 1769, by subscription.[17] The very large list of subscribers to it contains the names of many of the nobility and gentry of England, evidencing a very popular opinion of the merits of the work. It is doubly interesting to many persons in Western Pennsylvania, as the author was the great-great-grandfather of the Rev. Edward J. Knox, D. D., the esteemed pastor of the Methodist Episcopal Church of Beaver, who has kindly permitted me to use the map contained in it. This map, like the others, shows Logstown laid down in its proper relative position, on the north side of the Ohio.

4. Another map is that of Thomas Hutchins, an American Geographer, who, I think, accompanied the expedition of Col. Bouquet against the Ohio Indians in 1764. It places Logstown in the same position on the north side.

5. The next document is the journal of Col. Bouquet's march in October, 1764. His march was down the right or north bank of the Ohio. The entry of October 5th, states:

In this day's march the army passed through Logstown, situated seventeen miles, one-half and fifty-seven perches by the path from Fort Pitt. This place was noted before the last war for the great trade carried on there by the English and French, but its inhabitants, the Shawnese and Delawares, abandoned it in the year 1750.*

---

* This is probably a misprint for 1760, when Fort Pitt was finished. The journals of Croghan, Post and Washington show that Logstown was occupied from 1750 to 1760.

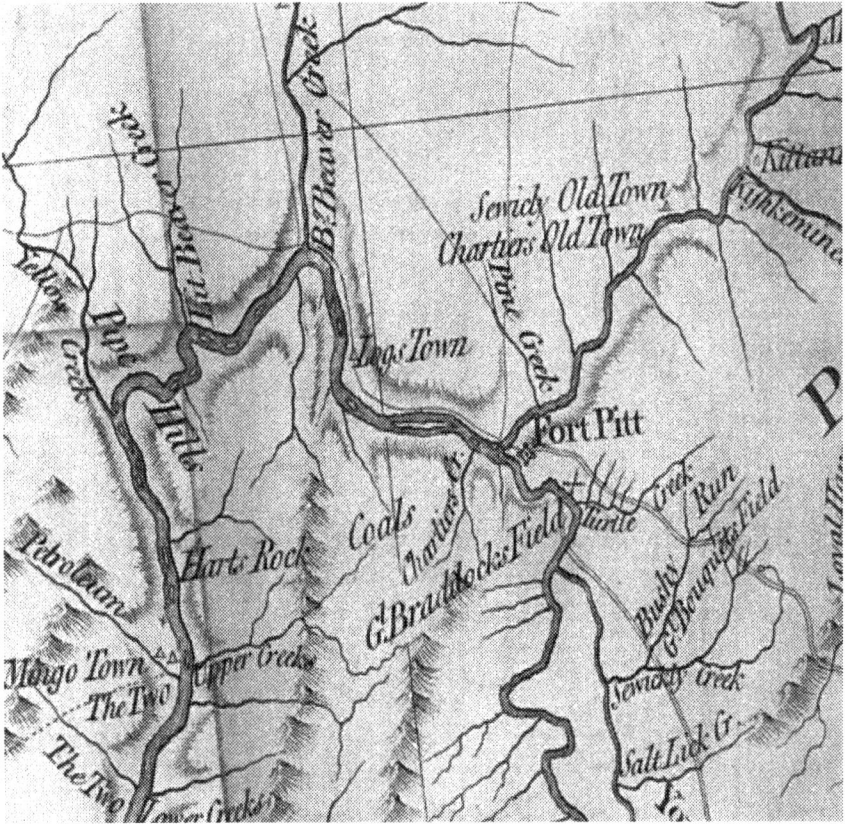

Detail from Thomas Hutchins, *A New Map of the Western parts of Virginia, Maryland and North Carolina,* London, 1778, showing the location of Logstown. Courtesy of the Library of Congress.

> The lower town extended about sixty perches over a rich bottom to the foot of a low steep ridge, on the summit of which, near the declivity, stood the upper town, commanding a most agreeable prospect over the lower and quite across the Ohio, which is about 500 yards across here, and by its majestic current adds much to the beauty of the place.

This description corresponds with that of Christian Frederick Post in his second journal.

119

6. Still another and conclusive document is the map of the Second District of Depreciation Surveys, made by Daniel Leet, in 1785 and 1786. This is a veritable record of the Land Office of Pennsylvania, on which hundreds of titles depend. In this map containing 143 lots surveyed on the north side of the Ohio, in the Second District, "Old Logstown" is laid down upon lots numbered 18 and 19, lying on the river. These are two tracts of land owned by the Harmony Society, at Economy. The Second (or Leets) District extended from the west side of the Big Beaver to the Big Sewickley creek, which, with the eastern line of the Second District, became the boundary between Allegheny and Beaver counties.

A feature of the Ohio may be noticed, as explaining some old references to lands on the east side of the Ohio. The general course of the Ohio from Pittsburgh to Beaver is northwest, but at Economy the river runs nearly due north, leaving the town and adjacent lands on the east side.

In considering these ancient journals which refer to the Indian nations, and the lands they occupied, especially viewing the old maps, which place before the eye so distinctly and so vividly the Indian countries, their boundaries, towns and cultivated valleys, one is struck with the number, density of population, and tribes of these nations, now wholly extinct. Men of to-day have no conception of their occupancy, power and rights. We are apt to look upon them as the merest nomads wandering over trackless forests, and tied to no homes. To this often is added the notion, like that in regard to the negroes of the south, they had no rights which white men were bound to respect. Yet when their condition at the time when the Europeans found them in possession, is considered, we must perceive that they were there rightfully, with title as good as that which generally invests nations with rights, and they felt the wrongs of those who are called civilized, yet with violence drove them from their homes and the graves of their people. The bow and arrow, and the stone hatchet were not equal to the musket and sabre, and might made right. It may have been, as some think, in the order of Providence, as lower orders of animals have given place to higher grades, that civilization was designed by an overruling Power, to prevail, by the extinction of the

Indian and the destruction of his rights. Yet this consummation, be it right or wrong, cannot repress sympathy for his fate, and a reflection that our own title rests on rapine and violence.

Notes:

[1] Logstown, or Chiningué, near Ambridge, PA, was first occupied by the Shawnee approximately 1725–1727. New Logstown was built by the French, most likely sometime in 1757 or 1758.

[2] Anthony Palmer (d. 1749) served on the council of Pennsylvania from 1708 until his death. As president of the council he served as acting governor in 1747–1748.

[3] Probably Queen Alequippa (d. 1754), the Seneca matriarch who at this time was living near the mouth of Chartier's Creek just below the Forks of the Ohio.

[4] The "Wandots" or "Owandots" were the Wyandot or Tionantanti Huron, who had moved to the Sandusky region of Ohio from Detroit. Weiser spent much of his time wooing the Wyandot from the French influence. The Tisagechroamis or Tisagechroanus were the Mississauga. For Weiser's Journal see *Pennsylvania Provincial Council Minutes, Colonial Records,* Vol. V, Harrisburg: Theo. Fenn & Co. 1851), pp. 348–358. It is also available on-line on the Glenn A. Black Laboratory of Archaeology website at www.gbl.indiana.edu.

[5] Philippe-Thomas Chabert de Joncaire (1707–circa 1766), French Indian agent, had accompanied Céloron de Blainville on his mission to the Ohio Valley in 1749. He was now back at Logstown with a small force of twelve men to woo the local tribes to the French cause. The French occupied the mouth of French Creek in 1753. For Joncaire see Malcolm MacLeod, "Philippe-Thomas Chabert de Joncaire," in *Dictionary of Canadian Biography On-line* at www.biographi.ca. For Croghan's letter, see "George Croghan to James Hamilton" in *Minutes of the Provincial Council of Pennsylvania, Colonial Records,* Vol. V, pp. 496–498. Available on-line at www.gbl.indiana.edu.

[6] The Twightwees were the Miami.

[7] All of these traders were active on the Ohio frontier. Thomas Kenton (circa 1689–1766) was a trader from Virginia and uncle of Simon Butler Kenton. Jacob Pyatt (b. 1703) was from Bedford County, PA. See notes at http://genforum.genealogy.com/pyatt, by Laverne Pyatt for his identification. Dennis Sullivan was in the employ of for Lazarus Lowry of Lancaster County, PA. John Prentice was taken prisoner by the Wyandot at Sandusky in 1763 and released at Detroit in 1764.

[8] Toanohiso, or Toanshiscoe was most likely Tanaghrisson (circa 1700–1754), the Half-King. He is believed to have moved to the Ohio in the 1740s and became the leading spokesman for the tribes. See William A. Hunter "Tanaghrisson," in *Dictionary of Canadian Biography On-line.*

Minutes of the Provincial Council of Pennsylvania, August 12, 1751, Colonial Records, Vol. V, pp. 530–539.

[9] Christian Frederick Post (1710–1785), Moravian missionary. His journal can be found in Reuben Gold Thwaites, *Early Western Journals, 1748–1765.*

[10] Killbuck or Smoky Island, was at the Forks of the Ohio. It was given to Gelelemend, or John Killbuck, Jr. (circa 1733–1811), for his services during the War of American Independence. He succeeded White Eyes as chief of the Turtle

Clan in 1778 and encamped on the island during the war. He sold his rights to the island for $200 in 1803. Most of the island was washed away in the flood of 1832. The channel was filled in during the late nineteenth century and what was left of the island is now part of the mainland. It is very probable that Croghan was actually referring to Gelelemend's father, John Killbuck, Sr. (died sometime in the 1770s), who was a prominent chief in the 1760s.

[11] Tawa was a commonly used name for the Ottawa.

[12] Shingas (died sometime after 1763) was chief of the Turtle Clan. He had led many raids against the frontier settlements during the French and Indian War.

[13] This was an obvious misprint as the correct date was November 24, 1758.

[14] Ketiuskund, or Keekyuscung, was a noted Delaware chief. His son was commonly referred to as "The Wolf." Both assisted British forces in their campaigns against the French in the Ohio River Valley, 1758–1760.

[15] Lieutenant Robert Hamilton of the 18th Regiment of Foot was serving in the garrison at Fort Pitt at this time.

[16] Lewis Evans (c. 1700–1756), a noted surveyor and geographer published *A General Map of the Middle British Colonies in America* in 1755.

[17] John Knox (d. 1778) of the 43rd Regiment of Foot served in Nova Scotia and at Quebec in 1759. He published *An Historical Journal of the Campaigns in North-America for the Years 1757, 1758, 1759 and 1760* (London, 1769).

Appendix:
Biographical Remarks

Abercromby, James (1706—1781)
James Abercromby arrived in North America in 1756 as second-in-command of British forces in North America under Lord Loudoun with the rank of major general. He assumed overall command in North America upon Loudoun's recall in March, 1758. He commanded the attack on Fort Ticonderoga, July 8, 1758, where he displayed a complete ineptitude for combat command and was soundly defeated. He was subsequently recalled and left for Great Britain in September, 1758. Abercromby was promoted to lieutenant general in 1759 and full general in 1772.

Agnew, Daniel (1809—1902)
Daniel Agnew was one of the earliest residents of Beaver, Pennsylvania. He graduated from Western University in Pittsburgh in 1825 and began to practice law. Agnew moved to Beaver in 1829. He became a member of the Whig Party and was appointed a judge in the 17th Judicial circuit in 1851. Agnew then served as a Justice of the Supreme Court of Pennsylvania from 1863–1878, and chief justice from 1873–1878. After his retirement, he returned to Beaver, where he spent most of the remainder of life in the pursuit of local history.

Allen, George
George Allen, along with Samuel Lightfoot and James Kenny opened a storehouse in Pittsburgh in 1759. He was present at a council with the Ohio tribes in July, 1759.

Allison, Richard (1757—1816)
Dr. Richard Allison served as surgeon's mate in the 5th Pennsylvania Regiment during the American War of Independence. He succeeded John McDowell as surgeon of the First Infantry Regiment in 1788. He was later promoted to surgeon of the general staff in 1792 and

served until 1796. After retiring from the service Allison settled in Cincinnati, Ohio where he went into private practice.

Allouez, Claude (1622–1689)
Claude-Jean Allouez was a French Jesuit missionary who had arrived in Canada in 1658. In 1667 he began missionary work in the region of Lake Superior and Lake Michigan centered around Green Bay in present-day Wisconsin. He later ministered to the Illinois and Miami tribes.

Amherst, Jeffery (1717–1797)
Amherst had served as an aide to General John Ligonier during the War of the Austrian Succession. He was commissioned lieutenant colonel of the 1st battalion of the 1st Foot in 1745 and acted as aide to the Duke of Cumberland at the Battle of Lauffeldt. He then served under the Duke of Cumberland in Germany in 1757. Ligonier promoted him to major general in America and chose him to command the Louisbourg campaign in 1758. William Pitt then appointed him commander-in-chief of British forces in North America, replacing Abercromby in September, 1758. He accepted the surrender of French forces in Montreal on September 8, 1760. In 1761 he ordered a new policy in dealing with the indigenous tribes by prohibiting the giving of gifts. This action has been noted as one of the primary causes of the Rebellion of 1763. Amherst returned to Great Britain in November, 1763. He was raised to the peerage as Baron Amherst in 1776 and was instrumental in quashing Gordon's Riots in London in 1780. He retired to his home in Kent in 1783.

Anderson, Robert
Anderson was commissioned an ensign in the Pennsylvania Regiment on December 5, 1757. He was serving as a lieutenant in the garrison at Fort Pitt in 1759.

Armstrong, John (1717–1795)
John Armstrong was commissioned a captain in the Pennsylvania Regiment in January, 1756 and lieutenant colonel in May, 1756.

He commanded the raid on the Delaware village of Kittanning on September 9, 1756 where he was wounded. In 1758 he commanded the 1st Battalion of the Pennsylvania Regiment on the Forbes Expedition. He later served in the Pennsylvania forces during the Rebellion of 1763. After the war Armstrong resided in Carlisle and served as a judge of the court of common pleas. He was commissioned a brigadier general in the Continental Army on March 1, 1776 and given command at Charleston, South Carolina. Armstrong was promoted to major general in 1777 and commanded the left wing of American forces at the Battle of Brandywine but did not actively engage in the battle. He subsequently held the line of the Schuylkill in an effort to delay the British advance. He also led a division of Pennsylvania troops at the Battle of Germantown where he failed to support Wayne and Sullivan. He resigned his commission in 1777 and was elected to the Continental Congress in 1778 where he served until 1780. He served again in 1787–1788. Armstrong died at Carlisle, PA in 1795.

Armstrong, John, Jr. (1755–1816)

The son of Major General John Armstrong, Armstrong served in the 3rd and 12th Pennsylvania Regiments during the War of American Independence. He later served in the West from 1784–1793 where he was stationed at Fort Pitt, 1785–1786 and at Fort Finney, 1786–1790. In 1790 he explored the lower Missouri and Wabash River Valleys. Anderson served with Harmar in 1790 and with St. Clair in 1791. He retired in 1793 and operated a store near Cincinnati, Ohio until 1807. Armstrong served as treasurer of the Northwest Territory from 1796–1802. He died in Clark County, Indiana in 1816.

Ashton, Joseph

Ashton served in the 1st Pennsylvania Artillery during the American War of Independence. He was serving in the 2nd Artillery Company in the garrison at Fort McIntosh in 1785.

Atlee, Samuel (1739–1786)

Atlee served as an officer in the Pennsylvania Regiment during the French and Indian War and rose to the rank of captain. During the

127

American War of Independence he served as colonel of the Pennsylvania Musketry Battalion until taken prisoner at the Battle of Long Island in 1776. He then served in the Continental Congress from 1778–1782. He was acting as an Indian commissioner in 1785.

Baldwin, Henry (1780–1844)

Henry Baldwin was a prominent attorney in Pittsburgh and a member of the U.S. House of Representatives 1816–1822. Daniel Agnew worked as a law student in his office during the 1820s. Baldwin served as a justice on the United States Supreme Court from 1830 until his death in 1844.

Barker, William

Barker took out a warrant in 1792 for lands along Walnut Bottom Run on which the town of Beaver Falls, Pennsylvania now stands.

Barrin de la Galissonière, Roland-Michel (1693–1756)

Barrin de la Galissonière served as governor of New France from 1747–1749. Prior to that he had a long career in the French Navy. During his tenure as governor he followed a defensive strategy against the expansion of British influence in North America, which included the dispatch of Pierre-Joseph Céloron de Blainville on a mission into the Ohio River Valley. Barrin de la Galissonière returned to France in 1749 and was appointed a commissioner to negotiate the boundaries between French and British territory in North America. He was placed in charge of the Department of Maps and Plans for the Navy in 1750 and was promoted to rear admiral on February 7, 1750. Barrin de la Galissonière was given command of a squadron in the Mediterranean Sea in early 1754 and was promoted to lieutenant general of naval forces on September 25, 1755. He was in command of the naval escort for the Maréchal de Richelieu's invasion of Minorca in 1756 and defeated Admiral John Byng at the Battle of Minorca on May 20, 1756, preventing the latter from relieving the besieged garrison. He died in France later that year.

Beatty, Erkuries (1759–1823)

Beatty served in the ranks and fought as a private at the Battle of White Plains and as a sergeant at the Battle of Long Island in 1776. He was promoted to ensign in the 4th Pennsylvania Regiment on January 3, 1777 and 1st lieutenant on May 2, 1777. Beatty was wounded at the Battle of Germantown. He was later appointed 1st lieutenant in the First American Regiment on July 24, 1784 and served as paymaster for the western army 1786–1788. Beatty served as commander of Fort St. Vincent, 1789–1790 and was promoted to major of the 5th Regiment of infantry in 1792. He resigned from the army in 1793.

Biddle, Edward (1738–1779)

Biddle was commissioned an ensign in the Pennsylvania Regiment on December 3, 1757. He was serving as a lieutenant in the garrison at Fort Pitt in 1759.

Bouquet, Henry (1719–1765)

Bouquet was a Swiss officer who entered the Dutch Army as a cadet in 1736. During the War of Austrian Succession he served with the Sardinian Army. In 1748, the Prince of Orange made him Captain Commandant of the Swiss Guards with the rank of lieutenant colonel. In the autumn of 1755 Bouquet accepted an invitation from the Duke of York to be lieutenant colonel of the 1st Battalion of the Royal American Regiment and left for North America in Spring, 1756. He commanded in Charleston, South Carolina in 1757 and was promoted to Colonel in North America in January, 1758. He served as second-in-command of Forbes' expedition in 1758 during which he ran the day-to-day operations of the army. In Pontiac's rebellion of 1763 he defeated the Ohio tribes at the Battle of Bushy Run on August 6, 1763, and raised the siege of Fort Pitt. He then commanded an expedition against the Delaware and Shawnee in 1764, negotiating a peace settlement without firing a shot in October, 1764. Bouquet was then promoted to brigadier general and placed in command of the southern colonies in 1765. He died, probably from Yellow Fever, shortly after his arrival in Pensacola, Florida, in September, 1765.

Brackenridge, Hugh Henry (1748–1816)

Brackenridge moved to Pittsburgh from Philadelphia in 1781 and founded the *Pittsburgh Gazette.* He was a representative in the Pennsylvania Assembly prior to serving as a judge from 1799–1814.

Braddock, Edward (1694–1755)

Braddock joined the Coldstream Guards as an ensign in 1710. He was promoted to lieutenant in 1716, lieutenant of grenadiers in 1727, captain lieutenant in 1734, captain in 1736, lieutenant colonel and 2nd major in 1743, and 1st major in May 1745. He commanded two battalions of the Coldstream Guards during the Scottish Revolt of 1745 but saw no action. Braddock was then promoted to lieutenant colonel in November 1745 and served in Flanders at Flushing in 1746–1747. He was named colonel of the 14th Foot in 1753 and acted as governor of Gibraltar, 1753–1754, and was commissioned a major general on March 29, 1754. Cumberland pronounced him commander in chief of British forces in North America in November 1754. He was mortally wounded at the Battle of Monongahela and died on July 12, 1755.

Brady, Samuel (1756–1795)

Brady served as a captain in the 8th Pennsylvania Regiment during the American War of Independence and later served as a scout. He commanded the scouts under General Anthony Wayne in 1792.

Brodhead, Daniel (1736–1809)

Brodhead's family had moved from New York to Bucks County, Pennsylvania in 1737. His family home was attacked by native warriors on December 11, 1755. He then served in the Pennsylvania forces throughout the French and Indian War. In 1773, Brodhead moved to Reading, where he was appointed deputy surveyor general. At the beginning of the Revolution he was appointed a delegate to the Pennsylvania Convention and raised a company of riflemen to fight with Washington. He was commissioned lieutenant colonel of the 4th Pennsylvania Regiment after the Battle of Long Island in 1776 and was then promoted to colonel of the 8th Pennsylvania in March, 1777.

His regiment the regiment was sent to Fort Pitt where he assumed command in April 1779. Shortly thereafter he commanded a swift raid up the Allegheny River to subdue the Delaware tribe in July 1779. When the Delaware again went on the warpath in spring 1781, Brodhead led a brutal strike against the friendly Delaware villages of Coshocton and Lichtenau in April. During his tenure in command Brodhead had made many influential enemies, including George Rogers Clark and Colonel John Gibson. He was court-martialed and acquitted, but General George Washington removed him from command. Brodhead was promoted to brigadier general after the war and retired to Milford, PA. He later served as surveyor general of Pennsylvania.

Brown, James

Brown was an Indian trader who was reported at Logstown in 1751.

Bryan, George (1731–1791)

George Bryan had come to Philadelphia from Dublin in 1752 and became a successful merchant. During the American War of Independence he served as vice-president of the supreme executive council of Pennsylvania in 1777 and became president of the supreme executive council in 1778. He later became an ardent anti-federalist.

Buade de Frontenac et de Palluau, Louis de (1622–1698)

Louis de Buade de Frontenac served twice as governor of New France. Prior to coming to North America he had risen to the rank of Marshal while serving in numerous campaigns on the continent. During his first administration from 1672–1682 he supported missions of exploration in the West by Jolliet and Marquette, La Salle, and others. He was soon embroiled in disputes with the Jesuits and other influential parties in New France and was recalled in 1682. Frontenac again served as governor from 1689–1698. His second administration was punctuated by war with the Iroquois, who made peace in 1696, and with the English. He died in office in 1698.

131

Butler, Richard (1743–1791)

Butler arrived in America from Ireland sometime before 1760. In 1777 he was serving as lieutenant colonel of Morgan's Rifle Corps. In 1783 he was acting as colonel of the 9th Pennsylvania Regiment. After the war he served as a commissioner for Indian affairs and negotiated the Treaty of Fort McIntosh. Butler was killed at St. Clair's defeat near present-day Fort Recovery, OH on November 4, 1791.

Campbell, Alexander (d. 1789)

Alexander Campbell was a resident of Pittsburgh who was killed in a raid by hostile Native American warriors on July 1, 1789.

Cavelier de La Salle, René-Robert (1643–1687)

Cavelier de La Salle is best known for being the first European to travel down the Mississippi from Canada to the Gulf of Mexico. His primary purpose was to explore the interior of the continent and establish a fur-trading network centered on his base along the Illinois River. In 1669–1670 he made an attempt to explore the Ohio River Valley. The French later cited his discovery as one of their primary claims to the Ohio Country. However, it is doubtful that he ever actually reached the Ohio River. Cavelier de La Salle died in Texas in 1687 while attempting to locate the mouth of the Mississippi River.

Céloron de Blainville, Pierre-Joseph (1693–1759)

Céloron de Blainville had long served in the *Troupes de la marine.* He entered the service as a cadet in 1707. He received a commission as 1st ensign in 1715. He was then promoted to Lieutenant in 1731 and captain in 1738. He served as commander at Fort Michilimackinac from 1734–1740. Céloron commanded the western detachment of French forces during their campaign against the Chickasaw in 1739–1740. He was placed in command at Fort Detroit in 1742, Fort Niagara in 1744, and Fort St. Frédéric in 1747. Céloron de Blainville commanded the expedition sent to explore the Ohio Valley and reestablish French dominance over the Ohio tribes in 1749. He left Montreal in June, traveled down the Allegheny River to the Ohio River and then up the Great Miami River to Fort des Miamis. Upon his return he noted the hostility of the local Indians and urged a fortified military presence on the Ohio. Shortly after his return he was named town major and commandant of Detroit. Céloron de Blainville was recalled in 1753 and named town major of Montreal where he died in 1759.

Chabert de Joncaire, Philippe-Thomas (1707–circa 1766)
Chabert de Joncaire was raised among the Iroquois. His father Louis-Thomas Chabert de Joncaire was the principal French agent to the Iroquois. Chabert de Joncaire was commissioned a 2nd ensign in 1727. He succeeded his father as agent among the Iroquois in 1739. He resigned his post in 1748 due to ill-health and returned to Montreal. However, in 1749 he returned to the frontier as interpreter, advisor, and second-in-command under Pierre-Joseph Céloron de Blainville on his mission to the Ohio River Valley. Chabert de Joncaire was next placed in command of a small garrison of twelve men sent to Chiningué (Logstown) in 1750 and was promoted to captain in 1751. He was placed in command of the post at the mouth of French Creek in June, 1753, where he oversaw construction on Fort Machault. He was relieved in June, 1755 and went to Fort Niagara. Chabert went to France after the war and died sometime in 1766 or before.

Champlain, Samuel de (1567–1635)
Champlain first came to North America as part of a trading voyage in 1603 and traveled up the Saint Lawrence River as far as the future site of Montreal. He then participated in the foundation of Port Royal in Acadia in 1605. He founded Quebec in 1608, discovered Lake Champlain in 1609, and traveled up the Ottawa River to Lake Huron in 1615. Champlain served as commander in New France from 1632 until his death in 1635.

Charles II (1630–1685)
Charles II reigned as King of England from 1669–1685. In 1681 he issued a grant of land roughly equal to the boundaries of the present State of Pennsylvania to William Penn.

Clapham, William, Jr. (d. 1763)

Clapham was commissioned a lieutenant in the battalion of his father, Lieutenant Colonel William Clapham of the Pennsylvania Regiment, on August 20, 1756. He was promoted to captain on April 23, 1760. He was serving under General Robert Monckton in the Ohio River valley in 1760. After the war he and his father settled on lands near Fort Pitt. They were both killed when Delaware and Mingo warriors attacked their estate on May 28, 1763, in one of the first raids of the Rebellion of 1763.

Clark, George Rogers (1752–1818)

Clark began working as a surveyor in present-day Kentucky in the early 1770s. He served as a captain of militia during Lord Dunmore's War in 1774. During the War of American Independence Clark became a leader among those who settled at Harrodsburg, Kentucky. While serving as a major of the Kentucky County militia he developed a plan to occupy the Illinois Country. He was appointed lieutenant colonel and given command of the expedition on January 1, 1778. Rogers captured Kaskaskia and Vincennes that summer. After Lieutenant Governor Henry Hamilton occupied Vincennes, Clark retook it in February, 1779 and took Hamilton prisoner. He next planned an attack on Fort Detroit but abandoned it. Clark was named brigadier general of the Virginia Militia in 1780. After the war he became Indian Commissioner of the Northwest Territory and also served on the commission appointed to oversee land grants in Indiana. In 1786 he led a failed expedition to subdue the Indians on the Wabash River and was dismissed. In 1788 he proposed settlement in Missouri and in 1791 was involved in plans to settle lands along the Yazoo River in Mississippi. He later proposed numerous other land schemes. Clark died in Locust Grove, Kentucky in 1818.

Clark, John (d. 1819)

Clark had served as an aide-de-camp to General Nathanael Greene. He was transferred to the 8th Pennsylvania Regiment on July 1, 1778 and served until the end of the war. He rejoined the army in 1791 and was wounded in St. Clair's defeat on November 4, 1791. He later rose to the rank of colonel.

Clayton, Asher

Clayton served as a lieutenant in the Pennsylvania Regiment and was promoted to captain lieutenant on December 1, 1757. He was serving as a captain in the 2nd Battalion, Pennsylvania Regiment in 1758 and fought in Grant's Defeat at Fort Duquesne on September 14, 1758. Clayton was in the garrison at Fort Pitt in 1759. He served as lieutenant colonel of the 2nd Battalion on Colonel Henry Bouquet's expedition to Ohio in 1764.

Connolly, John

Connolly was a doctor, trader, and land speculator. He was practicing medicine at Kaskaskia in 1768. By 1770 he was at Pittsburgh where he became a magistrate in the service of Virginia in October, 1773. As commander of Virginia forces at Fort Pitt he became a central figure in the dispute over control of the Pittsburgh region between Virginia and Pennsylvania. A Loyalist, Connolly fled the region at the outbreak of war in 1775.

Conrad, Nicholas

Conrad was commissioned an ensign in the Pennsylvania Regiment on December 29, 1755 and promoted to lieutenant on December 22, 1757. He was serving in the garrison at Fort Pitt in 1760.

Coulon de Villiers de Jumonville, Joseph (1718–1754)

Jumonville entered the *Troupes de la marine* as a cadet in 1733 serving under his father at Green Bay. He served in the campaign against the Chickasaw in 1739. Jumonville was commissioned an ensign in 1743 and served in Acadia in 1745–1746. In May 1754, He was given command of a small detachment sent to summon the English to depart from the Ohio Country. He was killed in Washington's surprise attack at what is now called Jumonville Glen on May 28, 1754. This skirmish contributed to the outbreak of the French and Indian War.

Craig, Isaac (1742–1826)

Craig arrived at Fort Pitt in April 1780 as commander of the artillery assigned to George Rogers Clark's abandoned expedition against

Fort Detroit. He was promoted to major in December, 1781. Craig settled in Pittsburgh after war and became a prominent businessman cofounding the first glass factory west of the Allegheny Mountains in 1791.

Crawford, Hugh (d. 1770)
Crawford was a Scot-Irish interpreter and Indian trader who was operating on the Pennsylvania frontier as early as 1739. During the French and Indian War he served as an ensign in the Pennsylvania Regiment and was serving in the garrison at Fort Pitt in 1760. Crawford was at Fort Ouiatenon near present-day Lafayette, Indiana in March, 1763 and was taken prisoner by the Wea when they captured the fort. He was exchanged in Illinois and arrived in New Orleans in December, 1763. He returned to Illinois in early 1765 but was forced to flee due to continued unrest among the Illinois tribes. Crawford was later employed by Sir William Johnson to escort Pontiac to Oswego in 1766.

Crawford, Robert
Crawford was commissioned an ensign in the Pennsylvania Regiment on April 24, 1758. He was serving in the garrison at Fort Pitt in 1760.

Croghan, George (circa 1720–1782)
Croghan was born in Dublin and immigrated to Pennsylvania in 1741. He soon became one of the most influential traders on the frontier, operating a trading house at Cuyahoga, or present-day Cleveland, Ohio, by 1747. He traded extensively with the Wyandot, Miami, Shawnee, and Delaware prior to the outbreak of the Seven Years' War. Croghan held an important council with the Ohio tribes at Logstown in May, 1751. During the war his home at Aughwick became a refuge for warriors allied with the British. Croghan was appointed deputy superintendent of Indian Affairs for the Pennsylvania and the Ohio tribes in November, 1756. In this capacity he held numerous councils with the tribes, several of them at Fort Pitt. Croghan was also a noted land speculator and used his official position to his advantage.

One of his greatest achievements was his peace treaties with the Wabash and Illinois tribes in 1765 and 1766. Croghan resigned from the Indian Department in 1772. A suspected Loyalist, he lost most of his extensive landholdings during the American War of Independence. He died in near poverty in 1782.

Croghan, William (b. 1754)

Croghan immigrated to North America and entered the Continental Army in 1776 as a captain in the Virginia Line. He participated in the Battles of Brandywine, Monmouth, and Germantown. In 1780 he was serving at Charleston, South Carolina where he was taken prisoner. After the war he immigrated to Kentucky and settled near the Falls of the Ohio. George Rogers Clark was his father-in-law.

Cuggens, Samuel

Cuggens was a trader who was at Logstown and attended Croghan's council there in May, 1751.

Dangerfield (Daingerfield), William (d. 1781)

Dangerfield was commissioned an ensign in the Virginia Regiment on September 3, 1755 and was promoted to lieutenant on May 25, 1757. He served in the 2nd Virginia Regiment in 1758 and was stationed at Fort Pitt in 1759. Dangerfield held the rank of captain lieutenant when the regiment was disbanded in 1762. He resided in Spotsylvania County until his death in 1781.

Dayton, Jonathan (1760–1824)

Dayton entered the 3rd New Jersey Regiment as an ensign in 1776 and served in the Mohawk River Valley. He was promoted to lieutenant in 1777 and fought at Brandywine and Germantown. He served in General John Sullivan's expedition to the Wyoming Valley in 1780. He was then promoted to captain in the 2nd New Jersey Regiment and served at Yorktown in 1781. After the war Dayton served in the New Jersey General Assembly 1786–1787. He served at the Constitutional Convention, 1787–1788, and was a signer of the Constitution of the United States. He served in the House of Representative as a

Federalist from 1791–1799 and served as Speaker of the House from 1795–1798. He then served as a senator from 1799–1804.

Denny, Ebenezer (1761–1822)

Denny had served as a dispatch rider between Carlisle and Fort Pitt. He also served for a short time as a privateer in the Caribbean before accepting a commission in the Pennsylvania line in 1780. He served at Yorktown in 1781 and kept a diary of the campaign. After the war he served in the First American Regiment from 1784–1791, rising to the rank of major. While serving in Fort McIntosh in 1785 he compiled a glossary of the Shawnee and Delaware languages. He later settled in Pittsburgh, became a banker, and was elected mayor in 1816.

Denny, William (1709–1765)

Denny was appointed Governor of Pennsylvania in August, 20, 1756. He worked for peace with the Delaware and Shawnee. He was re-called in 1759 after agreeing to sign a bill that allowed for taxation of the Penn family properties in Pennsylvania.

Dickinson, John (1732–1808)

Dickinson served as president of the supreme executive council of Pennsylvania from 1782–1785. He afterwards spent many years in Delaware politics and signed the United States Constitution as a delegate from Delaware.

Dinwiddie, Robert (1692–1770)

Dinwiddie was born in Glasgow in 1692 and attended Glasgow University. He began his career as a clerk in the customs office in Bermuda in 1721 and was named to the council of Bermuda in 1730. In 1738 he become collector of customs for Bermuda and was appointed surveyor general of customs for the southern colonies. He lived in Virginia for a short time in the early 1740s and was admitted to the Virginia Council in 1741. In December, 1743, Dinwiddie was serving in Barbados as inspector general. He returned to England in 1746 and was appointed lieutenant governor of Virginia in 1751.

He quickly became interested in western settlement and was a leader in urging British occupation of the Ohio River Valley. Dinwiddie was recalled and returned to England in January, 1758. He died at Bath on July 16, 1770.

Doughty, John (1754–1826)
Doughty joined the New Jersey artillery in 1776 and served as aide-de-camp to General Schuyler at Saratoga in 1777. Doughty was appointed fort major at West Point in 1782. He was sent to Fort McIntosh in 1785. Doughty resigned from the army in 1792 but again served as lieutenant colonel of the 2nd Regiment of Artillery and Engineers 1798–1800. He died in Morristown, NJ.

Douglass, Thomas
Douglass served in the 1st Pennsylvania Artillery during the American War of Independence. He was captain of the 2nd Artillery Company, First American Regiment, in 1784–1785.

Doyle, Thomas
Doyle was commissioned a lieutenant in the First American Regiment on August 12, 1784. He was serving as a captain in 1794 when he was sent by General Anthony Wayne to build Fort Massac at present-day Metropolis, Illinois.

Duncan, David
Duncan was an Indian trader who petitioned to be allowed to take control of Fort McIntosh when it was abandoned by the Army in 1785.

Duquesne de Menneville, Marquis Duquesne, Ange de (circa 1700–1778)
Governor of New France 1752–1755, Duquesne ordered the French occupation of the Ohio that led to the outbreak of the French and Indian War.

Edmonstone, Charles
Edmonstone was a captain in the 38th Regiment stationed at Fort Pitt.

Edmonstone was in command at Fort Pitt when General Thomas Gage ordered it abandoned in October, 1772.

Ellicot, Andrew (1754–1820)
Ellicot served as a commissioner to survey the boundaries of Western Pennsylvania in 1785. He was a highly regarded surveyor and astronomer and was appointed surveyor general of the United States in 1792. In 1797 Ellicot surveyed the boundary between the United States and Spanish Florida. In 1803 he trained Meriweather Lewis to survey in preparation for his exploration of the Louisiana Territory. In 1811 he surveyed the northern boundary of Georgia. In his later years Ellicot taught mathematics at West Point, where he died in 1820.

Elliot, Matthew (1739–1814)
Elliot was an Indian agent from Pittsburgh and associate of Alexander McKee and the Girty brothers. He fled Fort Pitt to join the British cause at Fort Detroit in March, 1777.

Evans, Lewis (c. 1700–1756)
Evans was a noted surveyor and geographer who published *A General Map of the Middle British Colonies in America* in 1755.

Few, William (1748–1828)
Few began practicing law in Augusta Georgia in 1776 and served as a member of the Georgia House of Representatives. He was a member of the executive council of Georgia in 1777–1778. Few was a member of the Continental Congress in 1780–1782 and again from 1786–1788. He served as a U.S. Senator from 1780–1793. Few moved to New York City in 1799 where he became active in local politics.

Finley, John
Finley served as a captain in the 8th Pennsylvania Regiment during the American War of Independence. When Fort McIntosh was abandoned in 1785 he and David Duncan petitioned for permission to occupy the site.

Finney, Walter (1747–1820)

Finney was taken prisoner at the Battle of Long Island 1776. He later served as a captain in the 6th Pennsylvania Regiment during the War of American Independence. He was commissioned a captain in the First American Regiment on August 12, 1784 and commanded at Fort McIntosh for a short time until the arrival of Colonel Josiah Harmar. He was serving as a major when he resigned his commission on September 1, 1787. Finney later served as a judge in Chester County, PA from 1790–1820.

Forbes, John (1707–1759)

Forbes was born in Scotland and studied medicine. He served as a quartermaster during the War of Austrian Succession and the Jacobite Rebellion. In 1755, he lobbied for the position of quartermaster in North America under Major General Edward Braddock but did not receive the position. He was promoted colonel of the 17th Foot in 1757 and served as adjutant general to John Campbell, Earl of Loudoun during the aborted Louisbourg expedition of 1757. Forbes was promoted to brigadier general in November, 1757 and given command of the expedition against Fort Duquesne in 1758. Although he was sick throughout entire campaign from liver and stomach disorders, he occupied the forks of the Ohio in late November, 1758. Forbes returned to Philadelphia shortly thereafter, where he died on March 11, 1759.

Fry, Joshua (1700–1754)

Fry was educated at Oxford as an engineer and cartographer. He immigrated to Virginia sometime prior to 1720 and became master of the grammar school at William and Mary College in 1729. He also served as a member of the House of Burgesses from 1744–1754. In 1751 he drafted a map of Virginia with the help of Peter Jefferson, father of Thomas Jefferson. Fry served as a delegate at the conference with the Ohio tribes at Logstown in May, 1752. Fry was commissioned colonel of the Virginia Regiment on February 25, 1754 but died in Alexandria, Virginia in May, 1754 from wounds he received after falling from his horse.

Gage, Thomas (1719–1787)

The second son of an Irish peer, Gage entered the army as an ensign sometime between 1736 and 1740. He was commissioned a lieutenant in January 1741, captain lieutenant in May 1742, and captain in January 1743. He was in Flanders in 1744 and served as an aide to the Duke of Albemarle from 1745–1748. Gage was promoted to major of the 44th Regiment in 1748 and was commissioned lieutenant colonel on March 2, 1751. He commanded the van of the British column at the Battle of Monongahela where he was wounded slightly in the belly. He served in New York in 1756 and on the aborted expedition against Louisbourg in 1757. In January, 1758, Gage became colonel of the 80th Light Infantry Regiment. Gage was acting as a brigadier general and was second in command at the Battle of Ticonderoga. He then commanded the rearguard of Amherst's army in 1760. He served as governor of Montreal 1760–1763 and was promoted to major general in 1761. Gage served as commander-in-chief of British forces in North America from 1763–1775 and commanded the British forces in Boston in 1774–1775. He was then recalled to Britain in October, 1775. Gage was promoted to full general in 1782 and died at the family estate of Portland Place, in Kent on April 2, 1787.

Gelelemend (John Killbuck, Jr.) (circa 1733–1811)

Gelelemend succeeded White Eyes as chief of the Turtle Clan of the Delaware Nation in 1778. He supported the American cause during the War of Independence and was deeded Killbuck's Island off Pittsburgh, where he settled. He sold his rights to the island in 1803.

Gibson, John (1740–1822)

Gibson has served as an ensign in the Forbes expedition and afterwards became a successful trader. He was taken prisoner by the Delaware in 1763 and released to Colonel Henry Bouquet in 1764. As colonel of the 13th Virginia Regiment, he was placed in command at Fort Laurens on 1788–1779. He served as commander at Fort Pitt for a short time in 1781.

Gilman (Gillman), Nicholas (1755–1814)

Gilman served as a member of the Continental Congress for New Hampshire in 1787–1789. He then served in the U.S. House of Representatives from 1789–1797 and as a U.S. Senator from 1805–1814.

Girty, George (1746–1796)

The brother of Simon Girty, he acted as an Indian agent for the British during and after the American War of Independence.

Girty, James (1743–1817)

The brother of Simon Girty, he acted as an Indian agent for the British during and after the American War of Independence.

Girty, Simon (1741–1818)

Girty's family was taken captive by a war party in 1756 and he spent three years in captivity among the Seneca. During the 1760s and 1770s he acted as a trader in the Ohio River Valley. Girty joined the British service as an interpreter in 1778 and participated in numerous raids on American settlers along the Ohio River throughout the remainder of the war. He settled on a farm near Amherstburg, Ontario after the war.

Gist, Christopher (1706–1759)

Gist was an Indian trader living in North Carolina in 1750 when he was hired by the Ohio Company to survey their western land grant in 1750–1751. He visited western Pennsylvania on the company's behalf in 1751–1752 and attended a council at Logstown in May 1752. In 1753, he began Gist's Settlement on the western side of Chestnut Ridge near present-day Brownsville, PA. Gist served as Washington's guide on his mission to the French forts on the Ohio in 1753. In 1754 he moved to Opechon, Maryland, across from the Wills Creek storehouse. Gist fought at the Battle of Great Meadows in 1754 and served as a scout on Braddock's expedition in 1755. He was appointed captain of the Virginia company of scouts in October, 1755. Gist was appointed deputy agent for Indian affairs in the southern department under Edmond Atkin in July 1757. He died of small pox in July 1759.

Gordon, Harry (d. 1787)
Gordon joined the Royal Engineers in 1742 and served under the Duke of Cumberland in Flanders in 1745 and again in 1747–1748. Considered a road-building specialist, Cumberland personally recommended he serve as an engineer under Braddock. He was assigned to St. Clair's working party and was wounded in the arm at the Battle of Monongahela. Gordon was attached to the 60th Regiment in 1756, and was commissioned engineer in ordinary and captain in January, 1758. He served under Forbes in 1758 and helped lay out his road through Pennsylvania. He also designed Fort Ligonier in 1758 and Fort Pitt in 1759. In 1766, Gordon traveled from Fort Pitt to Illinois and from there down the Mississippi to Mobile. He was promoted to major in 1773, lieutenant colonel in 1777, and colonel in 1782.

Graham, Arthur (d. 1789)
Arthur Graham was a resident of Pittsburgh who was killed in a raid by hostile Native American warriors on July 1, 1789.

Grant, James (1720–1806)
Grant was serving as major of the 77th Highlanders in 1758 when he commanded an advance party sent to raid Fort Duquesne. His force was soundly defeated on September 14, 1758 and he was taken prisoner. He then served as second-in-command on the expedition of 1760 against the Cherokee. He was given command of the expedition of 1761 and defeated the Cherokee at Cowee Mountain on June 10, 1761. Grant later served as governor of East Florida from 1763–1771. Grant returned to North America in 1776 as a brigadier general and commanded the left wing at the Battle of Long Island. In 1777 he was promoted to major general and commanded the right wing of the British Army at the Battle of Brandywine. In 1778 he commanded the expedition that captured the island of St. Lucia.

Greene, Nathanael (1742–1786)

Greene was appointed brigadier general of the Rhode Island brigade raised in 1776 to participate in the Siege of Boston. Greene also commanded the left wing at the Battle of Trenton. He also commanded the reserve at the Battle of Brandywine on September 11, 1777. In March 1778, Greene became quartermaster-general of the Continental Army. On June 28, 1778 he command the right wing at the Battle of Monmouth Courthouse. He resigned his position as quartermaster-general in 1780 and became commander at West Point. He was then placed in command of the southern theater and in 1781 commanded the American army at the Battles of Guildford Courthouse on March 15, Hobkirk's Hill on April 25, and Eutaw Springs on September 8.

Hamilton, Henry (circa 1734–1796)

Hamilton was commissioned an ensign in the 15th Regiment of Foot in 1755 and promoted to lieutenant in 1756. He served at the Siege of Louisbourg in 1758, and at Quebec in 1759. He was promoted to captain in 1762 and served at the Siege of Havana. Hamilton was in the garrison at Montreal in 1775 when he sold his commission and was appointed governor of Detroit later that year. After George Rogers Clark took Vincennes, Hamilton retook the fort in October, 1778. However, he was forced to surrender it to Clark again on February 25, 1779. He was taken prisoner and held in Virginia until 1781. He was then appointed lieutenant governor of Quebec 1782–1785 and later served as governor of Dominica from 1794 until his death in 1796.

Hamilton, James (1710–1783)

Hamilton began practicing law in Philadelphia in 1731 and succeeded his father Andrew Hamilton, as prothonotary of the Supreme Court of Pennsylvania in 1733. He was long active in Pennsylvania and Philadelphia politics and held several local offices including alderman and mayor of Philadelphia. He served three terms as lieutenant governor of Pennsylvania from 1748–1754, 1759–1763, and again for a short time in 1771. He died in New York in 1783.

Hamilton, Robert

Hamilton was a lieutenant in the 18th Regiment of Foot serving in the garrison at Fort Pitt in 1770. He accompanied George Washington on his trip down the Ohio River in 1770.

Hand, Edward (1744–1802)

Hand was born in Ireland and came to North America as a surgeon's mate in the British Army. He was commissioned a lieutenant colonel and commanded a Pennsylvania battalion during the siege Boston in 1775. He commanded at Fort Pitt with the rank of brigadier general from 1777 until 1780. He was then appointed adjutant general of the Continental Army in 1781. Hand was breveted major general in 1783 but resigned his commission shortly thereafter and retired to Lancaster, Pennsylvania.

Harmar, Josiah (1753–1813)

Harmar, a native of Philadelphia, entered the Continental Army as a captain in the 1st Pennsylvania Regiment in 1776. He was promoted to lieutenant colonel in 1777. He served under Washington from 1778–1780 and in the southern theater from 1781–1782. In 1783 he was breveted colonel of the First American Regiment and sent to Fort Pitt. He was present at the signing of the Treaty of Fort McIntosh with the Ohio tribes on January 20, 1785. Harmar was promoted to colonel on August 12, 1784 and breveted a brigadier general in 1787. Harmar became general of the army in 1789 and commanded an expedition against the Ohio tribes in 1790 that ended with his defeat near present-day Fort Wayne, Indiana on October 22. Afterwards, he resigned his commission and served as adjutant general of Pennsylvania from 1793–1799.

Heart, Jonathan (1748–1791)

Heart served as a captain in the First American Regiment from 1785–1791. He is probably best known for his description of the Native American mounds at Marietta, Ohio in 1791. He was killed at St. Clair's Defeat, November 4, 1791, on the banks of the Wabash River near present-day Fort Recovery, Ohio.

Heidler, Martin
Heidler was commissioned an ensign in the Pennsylvania Regiment on March 16, 1758. He was serving as a lieutenant at Fort Pitt in 1758.

Hemmington
He is listed as a member of the Committee of the Continental Congress appointed in 1788 to report on the status of the Department of War. He has not been identified.

Hennepin, Louis (1626—circa 1705)
Hennepin was a Recollet priest who arrived in Canada with La Salle in 1675. In 1676 he was at Fort Frontenac where he built a mission frequented by the Iroquois. Hennepin accompanied La Salle on his exploration of the Mississippi River in 1678–1680. In February, 1680, he was with a small party sent up the Mississippi River from Illinois. They were taken captive by the Sioux to their village in present-day Minnesota. Eventually released in September, 1680 the party made their way to Fort Michilimackinac. Hennepin returned to France in 1681 and wrote his *Description de la Louisiane,* popularizing his adventures and the exploits of La Salle.

Herbert, Stewart (1754–1795)
Stewart was commissioned an ensign in the 12th Pennsylvania Regiment on October 16, 1776. He was promoted to 2nd lieutenant on May 1, 1777 and then to 1st lieutenant on January 9, 1778. He was transferred to the 6th Pennsylvania Regiment on July 1, 1778 and was wounded and taken prisoner at Green Springs, Virginia on July 6, 1781. Stewart was commissioned 1st lieutenant and adjutant of the First American Regiment on August 12, 1784.

Hoofnagle, Michael
Hoofnagle was serving as a justice of the peace in Westmoreland County, Pennsylvania in 1783.

147

Howard, John Eager (1752–1827)

A native of Maryland, Howard served as a captain at the Battle of White Plains in 1776. He later fought at the Battles of Germantown and Monmouth as major of the 4th Maryland Regiment. In 1780 he was serving as lieutenant colonel of the 5th Maryland Regiment in South Carolina. Howard distinguished himself at the Battle of Cowpens in 1781 when he led the bayonet charge that secured the American victory. He also fought at Guilford Courthouse and Hobkirk's Hill in 1781. As colonel of the 2nd Maryland Regiment, he fought at the Battle of Eutaw Springs where he was severely wounded. After the war Howard began a successful political career. He served as a member of the Continental Congress in 1788 and governor of Maryland 1789–1791. He then served in the Maryland Senate from 1791–1795. He served in the United States Senate from 1796–1803. Howard ran for vice president of the United Stateson the Federalist ticket in 1816.

Hutchins, Thomas (1730–1789)

Hutchins was commissioned a lieutenant in the Pennsylvania Regiment, December 18, 1757 and served under Forbes in 1758. He was in the garrison at Fort Pitt in July, 1759. He was commissioned an ensign in the 1st Battalion, 60th Regiment of Foot on March 2, 1762 and served under Henry Bouquet on his expedition to Ohio in 1764 and served as an engineer. In 1766 he traveled down the Ohio and Mississippi Rivers touring the Illinois Country and West Florida. He returned to the Illinois Country in 1768. Hutchins eventually rose to the rank of captain and served as an engineer in West Florida 1772–1777. He left the British service in 1779 and returned to America where he was named Geographer of the United States in 1781. Hutchins published *A New Map of the Western parts of Virginia, Maryland and North Carolina* in 1778.

Irvine, William (1741–1804)

Irvine was a physician who immigrated from Ireland to Carlisle, Pennsylvania in 1763. He served as colonel of the 6th Pennsylvania Regiment and was taken prisoner in Canada on June 16, 1776. He was exchanged in May, 1779 and promoted to the rank of brigadier general on May 12, 1779. He commanded at Fort Pitt 1781–1783. Irvine served as a member of the Continental Congress 1786–1788. Irvine commanded the Pennsylvania forces during the Whiskey Rebellion, 1794. He then served in the U. S. House of Representatives, 1793–1795. He served as superintendent of military stores in Philadelphia from 1801 until his death in 1804.

Johnston, Francis (1748–1815)
Johnston served as colonel of the 5th Pennsylvania Regiment during the War of American Independence. He was a commissioner for the State of Pennsylvania at the Treaty of Fort McIntosh in February, 1785.

Jolliet, Louis (1645–1700)
As a young man Jolliet had entered the College of the Jesuits at Quebec in 1756, planning to enter the priesthood. He left the seminary in 1667 and became involved in the fur trade in 1668. In 1673, Jolliet, with Father Jacques Marquette, traveled down the Illinois River and explored the Mississippi River as far south as present-day Arkansas. He devoted most of the remainder of his life to the fur trade in northern Quebec.

Kennedy, John
Kennedy was commissioned an ensign in the Pennsylvania Regiment on December 23, 1757. He served as a lieutenant at Fort Pitt in 1759.

Ketiuscund (Keekyuscung, Kikyescund) (d. 1763)
A Delaware chief living at Kuskuskies in 1758, Ketiuscund and his son "The Wolf" actively aided Frederick Christian Post and the British after the capture of Fort Duquesne. Ketiuscund was reportedly killed at the Battle of Bushy Run on August 5–6, 1763.

Kenton (Kinton), Thomas (circa 1689–1766)
Kenton was a trader from Virginia active on the Pennsylvania frontier. He was present at Logstown during George Croghan's conference there in May, 1751. He was the uncle of the famous frontiersman Simon "Butler" Kenton.

149

Knox, Edward J.

Knox was pastor of the Methodist Episcopal Church in Beaver, Pennsylvania and a descendant of Captain John Knox.

Knox, John (d. 1778)

Knox entered the army as a cadet during the War of the Austrian Succession and was commissioned an ensign in the 43rd Regiment in 1749. He purchased a lieutenant's commission in 1754. Knox served garrison duty in Nova Scotia until 1759, when his regiment joined James Wolfe's expedition to Quebec. He participated in the Battle of Sainte-Foy on April 28, 1760, and was present at the capitulation of Montreal. From 1760–1761 he served as captain of an independent company that was incorporated into the 99th Regiment. He was placed on half pay when the regiment was disbanded in 1763. In 1769 he published *An Historical Journal of the Campaigns in North-America for the years 1757, 1758, 1759 and 1760.* In February 1775 Knox was placed in command of three independent companies at Berwick-upon-Tweed and held that command until he died in 1778.

Lamb, Caleb

Lamb was a trader who was present at Logstown during George Croghan's conference in May, 1751.

Laurens, Henry (1724–1792)

Laurens served as a representative in the South Carolina Congress in 1775 and was appointed its president. In November 1777 he was named president of the Continental Congress. In 1780 he was appointed a representative to Netherlands but was taken prisoner while crossing the Atlantic. Laurens was imprisoned in the Tower of London for fourteen months. After his release, he was appointed a minister for negotiating the peace in Paris and was one of the signers of the preliminaries of peace on November 30, 1782. His health shattered by his time in prison, Laurens retired to private life on his return to North America.

Le Caron, Joseph (circa 1586–1632)

Le Caron was a Recollet missionary who arrived in Canada in 1615. He was the first missionary to travel to the Huron Country in 1616. Most of his subsequent missionary work was with the Montagnais at Tadoussac, Quebec. He returned to France in 1625.

Lee, Arthur (1740–1792)

Lee was the youngest son of Thomas Lee. He had served as agent in London for the colony of Massachusetts prior to the War of American Independence. During the war he served as a commissioner to France in 1776 and to Spain in 1777. Lee served in the Continental Congress 1782–1784. He served as a commissioner for the United States at the Treaty of Fort McIntosh in February, 1785.

Lee, William

Lee served as a sergeant in the 8th Pennsylvania Regiment during the American War of Independence. He was serving as a sergeant at Fort McIntosh in 1783.

Leet, Daniel (1748–1830)

Leet served as a quartermaster, paymaster, and brigade major during the War of American Independence. He also served as second-in-command on William Crawford's expedition against the Ohio Indians in 1782. After the war he settled at Chartier Creek and became a surveyor in Western Pennsylvania. Leet served in the General Assembly of Pennsylvania in 1791–1792.

Lightfoot, Samuel (d. 1759)

Lightfoot and his partner James Kenney opened a storehouse in Pittsburgh in 1759. He died there on July 30 of that year.

Ligonier, John, 1st Earl Ligonier (1680–1770)

Ligonier was a Huguenot whose family immigrated from France to Great Britain in the late seventeenth century. He joined the British Army as a volunteer in 1702 and participated in most of the major battles and campaigns during the War of the Spanish Succession including Blenheim, Ramillies, Oudenarde, and Malplaquet. He was appointed governor of Fort St. Philip on Minorca in 1712. Ligonier was appointed colonel of the 7th Dragoons in 1720, promoted to brigadier general in 1735, and major general in 1739. He then served as an advisor to the Duke of Cumberland during the War of Austrian Succession. Ligonier succeeded Cumberland as commander-in-chief of the British Army in 1757.

Lochry, Archibald (1733–1781)

During the Rebellion of 1763 Lochry served with the Pennsylvania Regiment. He later became county lieutenant of Westmoreland County, Pennsylvania and was actively involved in the defense of the Pennsylvania frontier during the War of American Independence. He led a detachment of 106 militia down the Ohio River in 1781 to join up with George Rogers Clark for a proposed expedition against Detroit. Native American warriors ambushed his party near the mouth of present-day Laughery Creek in Dearborn County, Indiana on August 24. Lochry was killed and his entire detachment was either killed or taken prisoner.

Louis XV (1710–1774)

Louis XV reigned as King of France from 1715 till 1774.

Lowry, Alexander (1723–1805)

Lowry was a highly successful Indian trader on the Ohio frontier beginning in the 1740s. Lowry served as a messenger for the commissioners organizing the council at Fort McIntosh in January, 1785. He also had a long career in Pennsylvania politics, serving on the committee of correspondence in 1774, in the general assembly 1775–1776, and in the state senate from 1785–1788.

Lyon, James

As a boy Lyon was taken prisoner by Native American warriors in 1782 on Turtle Creek, Westmoreland County, Pennsylvania. He was released at Fort McIntosh in 1785 per the terms of the Treaty of Fort McIntosh. He opened a store in Beaver, Pennsylvania in 1800 and served as Beaver County sheriff, 1818–1821.

Marquette, Jacques (1637–1675)

Marquette was a Jesuit priest who arrived in Canada in 1766. In 1668 he began missionary work at Sault Sainte Marie and in 1669 founded a mission at Chequamegon Bay in northern Wisconsin. He accompanied Jolliet on his exploration of the Illinois and Mississippi Rivers in 1673. He returned to the Illinois in 1674–1675 to found a mission, but became ill. He died while returning to St. Ignace on the Upper Peninsula of Michigan.

Matthews, Edmond

Matthews was commissioned an ensign in the Pennsylvania Regiment on March, 14, 1757. He was serving as a lieutenant at Fort Pitt in 1759 but was discharged from service before the beginning of the 1760 campaign.

McClean, Alexander (1746–1834)

McClean was a surveyor from Uniontown, Pennsylvania. He led the survey to complete the Mason-Dixon Line in 1782. In 1785, McClean surveyed the boundaries of the Beaver Reservation for the Pennsylvania government.

McClure, John

McClure served as a sergeant in the 8th Pennsylvania Regiment during the American War of Independence. He was serving as a sergeant at Fort McIntosh in 1783.

McCurdy, William

McCurdy served as a captain in the First American Regiment from 1784–1791.

McDowell, John (1745–1825)

McDowell served as an officer and surgeon in the 2nd Pennsylvania and 6th Pennsylvania Regiments from 1776–1783. He then served as surgeon of the First American Regiment from 1784–1788. He was residing in Greensburg, Pennsylvania when he died.

McDowell, Nathan

McDowell was serving as an ensign the the First American Regiment garrisoned at Fort McIntosh in 1785. He was a signatory of the treaty with the Shawnee at the mouth of the Great Miami River in January 1786. McDowell served under Colonel Josiah Harmar on the Wabash River in 1787 and accompanied him to Kaskaskia, Illinois. He was serving as a lieutenant in command at the Big Beaver Blockhouse in present-day New Brighton, Pennsylvania in 1789.

McIntosh, John Mor

McIntosh arrived in Georgia from Scotland in 1736 and settled in present-day Darien, Georgia. He served under Oglethorpe in Florida in 1740 and was taken prisoner to Spain. He was released in 1742 and died a few years later. He was the father of Lachlan McIntosh.

McIntosh, Lachlan (1725–1806)

The son of John Mor McIntosh, he became a clerk in Charleston, South Carolina at age seventeen. He then returned to Georgia and became a surveyor and engineer. McIntosh was appointed a brigadier general in September, 1777. He commanded the Western Department in 1778–1779 and ordered the construction of Fort McIntosh during his tenure. He was recalled in 1779 to serve in the south, commanding at the siege of Savannah, Georgia. He served in the Continental Congress in 1784 and as a commissioner to treat with the southern tribes in 1785.

McIntyre, Thomas

McIntyre served as captain of an independent company in Western Pennsylvania during the War of American Independence until May, 1782.

McKee, Alexander (circa 1735–1799)

McKee was the son of trader Thomas McKee. His mother was said to be the Shawnee, Tecumsapah. He was commissioned a lieutenant in the Pennsylvania Regiment on December 17, 1757. He joined the Indian Department as an assistant to George Croghan in 1760.

During the 1770s he married into the Shawnee tribe and lived with them on the Scioto River. McKee fled Fort Pitt for Detroit in March, 1778 to serve the British. He became a captain and interpreter in the Indian Department and had great influence among the Ohio tribes. During the remainder of the War of American Independence he participated in numerous raids against the frontier settlements. After the war he settled on the Canadian side of the Detroit River and continued to serve as a deputy in the Indian Department actively encouraging the Ohio tribes to continue their war against the United States.

McKee, Thomas (circa 1695–1769)
Mckee was born in Ireland and immigrated to Pennsylvania, where he opened a trading post at McKee's Falls on the Susquehannah River in 1742. He served as a captain in the Pennsylvania Regiment during the French and Indian War. After the war he served as an assistant in the Indian Department to George Croghan.

McNeill, John (d. 1765)
McNeill was commissioned an ensign in the Virginia Regiment on December 4, 1754 and served on the Braddock expedition. He was promoted to lieutenant on August 18, 1755 and accompanied the Sandy Creek Expedition in February, 1756. McNeill was promoted to captain lieutenant of Colonel George Washington's company on July 21, 1756. He was promoted to captain in October 1757. In 1760 he served in the detachment sent to Presqu'Île. He was promoted to major of the Virginia Regiment in May, 1762. McNeill served as colonel of the Augusta County militia on Colonel Henry Bouquet's march to Ohio in 1764. He fell sick during the expedition and died in February, 1765.

Mercer, Hugh (1726–1777)
Mercer was born in Scotland and was in training to become a surgeon in 1745 when he joined the Jacobite Army as a physician's assistant. Mercer is said to have fled to Pennsylvania in 1746 where he practiced medicine in the back country for several years. He was commissioned a captain in the Pennsylvania Regiment in March, 1756,

promoted to major in 1757, and colonel in May, 1758. Mercer was placed in command at Fort Pitt in December, 1758. He continued to serve on the Pennsylvania frontier until the end of the 1760 campaign. He moved to Fredericksburg, Virginia in 1761 where he continued to practice medicine until the American War of Independence. In late 1775, Mercer was named colonel of the 3rd Virginia Regiment. He died on January 12, 1777 from wounds received at the Battle of Princeton.

Mésnard, Réné (1605–1661)
Mésnard was a Jesuit missionary who traveled west in 1660 to establish a mission at Chequamegon Bay, (present-day La Pointe, Wisconsin). He was abandoned on the shore of Lake Superior en route. In 1661 he traveled alone up the Blackwater River in Wisconsin and was never heard from again.

Michel, Joseph (d. 1788)
Michel was reported killed in July, 1788 while traveling down the Ohio River twenty miles below the mouth of the Big Miami River.

Miles, Samuel (1739–1805)
Miles was commissioned an ensign in the Pennsylvania Regiment on May 24, 1756, and lieutenant on December 14, 1757. He was promoted to captain on April 21, 1760 and served in the detachment sent to Presqu'Île that summer. After the war he went into business as a merchant in Philadelphia and served in the General Assembly, 1772–1774. He commanded a regiment of riflemen in 1776 and was taken prisoner at the Battle of Long Island. During his imprisonment he was promoted to brigadier general. Miles was exchanged in April, 1778. He then served as deputy quartermaster general for Pennsylvania until 1782. After the war he served as a judge and an alderman, and became mayor of Philadelphia in 1790. He was a Federalist delegate to the Electoral Congress in 1796.

Minis, David
A former resident of Beaver, Pennsylvania. He owned the land on which the village of Sawkunk had been located.

156

Monckton, Robert (1726–1782)

Monckton was commissioned in the 3rd Foot Guards and served in Flanders during the War of Austrian Succession. He participated in the battles of Dettingen and Fontenoy. He was commissioned a captain in the 34th Regiment on June 27, 1744, major on February 15, 1748, and lieutenant colonel of the 47th Regiment on February 28, 1752. In August, 1752, Monckton was placed in command of Fort Lawrence in Nova Scotia. He commanded the army that captured Fort Beauséjour on June 16, 1755 and oversaw the expulsion of the Acadians from Nova Scotia later that year. He served as a brigadier general under James Wolfe in 1759 and commanded the right wing at the Battle of Quebec on September 13. He was then promoted to colonel of the 17th Regiment in October, 1759. Monckton was named commander of British troops in the southern colonies on April 29, 1760 and served until early 1761 when he was promoted to major general and placed in command of the expedition against Martinique. He returned to England in 1763 and was promoted to lieutenant general in 1770.

Montour, Catherine (Elizabeth Couc) (circa 1667–1750)

Little is known of Montour's early life. Her given name itself is shrouded in mystery but it is believed she was the Elizabeth Couc who was born in Trois Rivières in 1667. About 1695 she was captured by the Iroquois. She was later ransomed by her brother-in-law Maurice Ménard and accompanied him to Michilimackinac. She later joined her brother Louis Couc Montour in New York and by 1709 was referring to herself as Madame Montour. She worked as an interpreter for the colony of New York and married the Oneida Chief Carundawana (Robert Hunter). In 1727 she attended a conference in Philadelphia and resided in Pennsylvania for the rest of her life. She lived at the present site of Williamsport, Pennsylvania from 1737–1742 and was at Sunbury in 1745. She was reported at Harris's Ferry in October, 1748 but apparently died a short time later. She was the mother of Andrew Montour. Montour County, Pennsylvania was named after her.

Montour, Andrew (Henry) (circa 1707–1774)

The son of Catherine Montour, Andrew worked for Conrad Weiser as an interpreter from 1744–1756 and accompanied George Croghan and William Trent to Logstown in 1751 and 1752. He served with Edward Braddock in 1755. He resided on Montour Creek at the mouth of Sherman Creek a few miles northwest of Carlisle.

Morgan, Jacob, Sr. (1716–1792)

Jacob Morgan, Sr. was commissioned a captain in the Pennsylvania Regiment on December 18, 1757. He served in the garrison at Fort Pitt in 1759. He later served as county lieutenant of Berks County, Pennsylvania.

Morgan, Jacob, Jr. (1742–1802)

Morgan was commissioned an ensign in his father's company of the Pennsylvania Regiment on March 12, 1758. He served with his father at Fort Pitt in 1759. He was promoted to lieutenant and adjutant on April 21, 1760. Morgan served as a colonel in the Pennsylvania Line during the War of American Independence.

Murray, John, 4ᵗʰ Earl of Dunmore (1732–1809)

Dunmore was a descendant of the Stuart line of kings. He succeeded his father as 4ᵗʰ Earl of Dunmore in 1765. In 1761 and 1768 he was elected one of the Scottish peers to serve in Parliament. He was appointed governor of Virginia in 1771. Dunmore soon became heavily involved in western expansion. In 1774 he led the Virginia forces in the war against the Ohio tribes that became known as Lord Dunmore's War. He also supported Virginia's claim to Western Pennsylvania and ordered Captain John Connolly to occupy Fort Pitt in 1774. Dunmore took refuge aboard a British man-of-war at the outbreak of the War of American Independence in 1775. In 1776 he commanded a detachment of loyalists and conducted raids along the James and York Rivers in Virginia. He later became governor of Bermuda in 1786.

Nelson, Joseph

Nelson was acting as a trader on the Ohio frontier in the early 1750s. He was present at Logstown during the council of May, 1751.

Neville, John (1731–1803)

Neville served in Lord Dunmore's War in 1774 and received a grant of land on Chartier Creek for his services. He was elected to the Virginia Convention in 1774 but was too ill to attend. He commanded the Virginia militia at Fort Pitt from September, 1775 to 1777. Neville eventually rose to the rank of Brigadier General and served prominently in the Whisky Rebellion.

Neville, Joseph (1730–1819)

Neville had served in the House of Burgesses for Hampshire County, 1773–1776. He also served in the Virginia Conventions of 1775 and 1776. In 1782 he helped complete the survey of the Mason-Dixon Line and was appointed surveyor of Hampshire County, Virginia in 1784. In 1785 he served as a member of the commission that surveyed the western boundary between Virginia and Pennsylvania. Neville later served in the United States Congress from 1793–1795. He died in Moorefield, West Virginia.

Oglethorpe, James (1698–1785)

Oglethorpe had joined the army in 1714. He served as an aide-de-camp to Prince Eugene of Savoy in the Turkish campaign of 1716–1717 and was present at the Siege of Belgrade. He became a member of Parliament in 1722 and soon became interested in reforming the debtors' prison. He believed that debtors needed a new start on life and began lobbying that they be released to settle a new colony. Oglethorpe and 35 families founded the city of Savannah in 1733 creating the new colony of Georgia. Relations between Georgia and the Spanish in Florida were strained, and when the War of Jenkins' Ear broke out, Oglethorpe commanded an unsuccessful attempt to capture Saint Augustine. He then commanded the defense against a Spanish attack on Georgia in 1742. He returned to Britain in 1743. In 1745 Oglethorpe was promoted to major general and assigned to attack Prince Charles Edward's Highland army. He failed to engage them and was subsequently court-martialed, but acquitted. He turned the charter of Georgia over to the King in 1752 and retired from Parliament. Oglethorpe was given the opportunity to take command of the British Army in North America after the recall of General Thomas Gage in 1775, but he declined.

O'Hara, James (d. 1819)

O'Hara was born in Ireland and entered the Royal Navy as an ensign. He soon left the navy and immigrated to Pennsylvania where he became a trader at Fort Pitt in late 1773. He became an Indian agent in March, 1774. He commanded an independent company garrisoned on the Kanawha River until 1779. O'Hara then served as commissary to the General Hospital in Carlisle, Pennsylvania in 1779–1780. After that he became assistant quartermaster general under General Nathanael Greene in the south. He returned to the mercantile trade after the war until April 19, 1792, when he was appointed quartermaster general under General Anthony Wayne and served in that capacity until 1796. O'Hara was also a signatory to the Treaty of Greenville on August 3, 1795. He settled in Pittsburgh and later became a president of the Bank of Pennsylvania. His daughter, Mary O'Hara, married William Croghan.

O'Hara Croghan, Mary

The daughter of James O'Hara of Pittsburgh. She married William Croghan, who was a frequent visitor to the law office of Henry Baldwin, where author Daniel Agnew worked as a clerk in the 1820s.

Ormsby, John (1720–1805)

Ormsby came to North America from Ireland in 1752. He served as a commissary under General John Forbes in 1758. He settled in Pittsburgh after the French and Indian War and engaged in the fur trade. He was present at the Siege of Fort Pitt in 1763. Ormsby became a leading early citizen of Pittsburgh.

Owens, John

Owens was a trader operating on the Pennsylvania frontier in the early 1750s. He was present at George Croghan's council of May, 1751 at Logstown.

Palmer, Anthony (d. 1749)

Palmer served on the council of Pennsylvania from 1708 until his death in 1749. As president of the council he served as acting governor in 1747–1748.

Pearce, Paul

Pearce was trading at Logstown in 1751 and was present at the council held there in May by George Croghan.

Pécaudy de Contrecoeur, Claude-Pierre (1706–1775)

Pécaudy de Contrecoeur was commissioned an ensign in the *Troupes de la marine* in 1729, was promoted to lieutenant in 1742, and captain in 1748. In 1749 he accompanied Jean-Baptiste Céloron de Blainville on his mission down the Ohio River. He served as commandant at Fort Niagara from 1752–1754. He was named commander of French forces in the Ohio Country in early 1754 and occupied the forks of the Ohio River in April of that year. Pécaudy de Contrecoeur commanded at Fort Duquesne until relieved in late 1755. He was awarded the Cross of the Order of Saint-Louis in March, 1756. Pécaudy de Contrecoeur resigned his commission in 1759. He later became a leader of the French party during the British Régime and was appointed to the Legislative Council of Quebec in 1774.

Penn, William (1644–1718)

In 1682, Penn received a charter from Charles II, granting him the proprietorship of what would become the colony of Pennsylvania. He had converted to the Quaker faith in 1667 and founded the colony as a haven for those practicing the Quaker faith.

Peters, Richard (1704–1776)

Peters was born in Liverpool, England and became an ordained Anglican minister approximately 1731. He immigrated to Philadelphia in 1735 and served as assistant minister at Christ Church until 1737 when he became secretary to the province of Philadelphia. He held this position until 1762, when he resigned to officiate over the united churches of Philadelphia as rector. He resigned in 1775. Peters was also a member of the provincial council until his death in 1776.

Pitt, William (1708–1778)

Pitt entered Parliament in 1735 and soon became a leader of the opposition against the government of Robert Walpole. He was appointed Secretary of War in 1757 and given control over British War plans. He resigned in late 1761 when the majority of the Cabinet refused to back his call for a declaration of war against Spain. Elevated to the peerage as the Earl of Chatham, he briefly led a second, mostly ineffectual ministry in 1766–1768.

Pontiac (circa 1720–1769)

Pontiac's youth is obscure but it has been said he was born along the Maumee River of a Ojibwa mother and Ottawa father. He is also said to have fought at the Battle of Monongahela on July 9, 1755. By 1760, he was a leading chief among the Ottawa, Ojibwa, and Potawatomi tribes. In that year he made peace with the British. His disposition had changed by 1762 due to a lack of trade goods and supplies. Perhaps swayed by the Delaware sachem Neolin, Pontiac urged war in a council at Rivière â l'Écorce on April 27, 1763. Pontiac besieged Fort Detroit on May 9. On July 29, he defeated a detachment led by Captain James Dalyell at Bloody Run. As the siege continued Pontiac's forces dwindled. When he learned in October, 1763 that the French and English had finalized the peace, he withdrew to Illinois seeking French aid. He failed to obtain assistance but managed to arouse the Illinois tribes. He eventually agreed to a preliminary peace with George Croghan at Fort Ouiatenon in July 1765 and met with William Johnson in July 1766 at Fort Ontario for a final treaty. When dissatisfied factions sought his aid in 1767 he was banished from his village even though he proclaimed continued loyalty to the British. He eventually made his way back to Illinois where he caused much anxiety among the Kaskaskia and the local inhabitants. In April, 1769, the Peoria held a council and decided Pontiac must die. The assassination was carried out by Makatachinga on April 20, while Pontiac was in Cahokia, Illinois to trade furs.

Porter, Andrew (1743–1813)
Prior to the War of American Independence Porter had taught mathematics in Philadelphia. He was commissioned a captain in the marines in 1776 and transferred to the artillery shortly thereafter. Porter fought at the Battles of Princeton, Brandywine, Germantown, and on John Sullivan's Expedition and had risen to the rank of colonel of the 4th Pennsylvania Artillery by the end of the war. He served on the commission to survey the boundary of Western Pennsylvania in 1785. Porter eventually rose to the rank of major general and served as surveyor general of the United States from 1809–1813.

Post, Frederick Christian (1710–1785)
Born in Prussia, Post came to Pennsylvania in 1742 as a Moravian missionary. Between 1743–1749 he ministered to Moravian converts in New York and Connecticut. He returned to Germany in 1751 and spent a short time in Labrador. He was back in Pennsylvania in 1758, at which time he undertook an embassy to the Ohio Country to convince the Delaware and Shawnee nations to make peace. He kept journals of his two trips to the Ohio. After the French were defeated, he established a mission in the Ohio Country in 1761 but was forced to abandon it during the Rebellion of 1763. Post then left for the Mosquito Coast in the Caribbean, where he labored from 1764–1767.

Prentice, John
Prentice was a trader who was present at Logstown during the council held by George Croghan in May, 1751. He was commissioned a lieutenant in the Pennsylvania Regiment on December 6, 1757 and was promoted to captain in March, 1759. After the war he returned to the western trade. Prentice was trading with the Wyandot at

Sandusky, Ohio at the outbreak of the Rebellion of 1763 and was taken prisoner. He was released at Fort Pitt in 1764.

Pyatt, Jacob (b. 1703)
Pyatt was a member of a family of traders from Bedford County Pennsylvania and was the second to carry the name "Jacob." He was noted at Lancaster, Pennsylvania in 1734. Pyatt was present in Logstown at the council held there by George Croghan in May, 1751. He is believed to have operated a trading post in Path Valley.

Reed, Joseph (1741–1785)
Born in New Jersey, Reed graduated from Princeton in 1757 and moved to England for further studies and to practice law. He returned to Philadelphia and was appointed to the committee of correspondence. He served as a delegate to the 1st Continental Congress. He then served as an aide-de-camp and secretary to General George Washington in 1775. He became adjutant general in 1776. Reed was appointed chief justice of Pennsylvania and commissioned a major general in 1777. He served as president of the supreme executive council of Pennsylvania 1778–1781.

Rittenhouse, David (1732–1796)
Rittenhouse was a well-known surveyor, mathematician, inventor, and astronomer, as well as a member of the American Philosophical Society. He invented the Rittenhouse compass, which was used by surveyors until the mid-nineteenth century. He helped complete the Mason-Dixon Line in 1784. He was one of the commissioners who surveyed the southwestern boundary of Pennsylvania in 1785. He became the first director of the United States Mint from 1792–1795.

Rosenthal, Gustavus Henri de, Baron (John Rose)
Rosenthal was a Russian nobleman who had fled to North America after killing another nobleman in Russia. He took the alias John Rose and joined the American cause becoming surgeon in the 7th Pennsylvania Regiment. Rosenthal served in the navy for a time then became

aide-de-camp to General William Irvine. He returned to Russia in 1784.

Saint Clair, Arthur (circa 1734–1818)
Saint Clair was born in Scotland and entered the British Army as an ensign in 1757. He served at Louisbourg in 1758 and at Quebec in 1759. He resigned his commission in 1762 and settled in Pennsylvania where he held several positions under the proprietors. During the American War of Independence he served in Canada in 1775. He was promoted to brigadier general in 1776. In 1777 he was promoted to major general and placed in command at Fort Ticonderoga. He then served in the Continental Congress 1785–1787. Saint Clair served as the first governor of the Northwest Territory from 1787–1802. In 1791 he commanded an army sent to defeat Native American forces on the Upper Wabash. He was ambushed on November 4 near present-day Fort Recovery, Ohio and defeated.

Schenley, Mary Croghan (1826–1903)
Mrs. Schenley was the daughter of William Croghan and Mary O'Hara Croghan. In 1841, at age 16, she eloped with 43-year old Captain Edward W. Schenley of the British Army. The elopement caused quite a sensation in Pittsburgh and Washington, DC at the time. She died in England in 1903.

Shepherd, David (1734–1795)
Shepherd settled at the forks of Wheeling Creek about 1774. He commanded Fort Henry in 1777. He later served as county lieutenant of Ohio County, VA, and served in the Virginia legislature.

Shingas (d. 1763)
Shingas was chief of the Turkey Division of the Delaware tribe and the brother of Tamaqua. In 1752 he founded Shingastown at the mouth of the Big Sandy Creek on the Tuscarawas River near present day Bolivar, Ohio and was considered leader of the Ohio Delaware. He was living at the mouth of Chartier Creek in 1753 and guided George Washington to Logstown. He remained friendly toward the

British when the French arrived and attempted to maintain the neutrality of his people until the Battle of Monongahela in July, 1755. After Braddock's defeat, he went over the French side and became the leader of many devastating raids on the Pennsylvania, Maryland, and Virginia frontier. Shingas made peace with General John Forbes at Fort Duquesne in November 1758. In May 1763, he and other chiefs warned trader Thomas Calhoun to flee his post on the Tuscarawas. When Calhoun's party was ambushed at the mouth of Beaver Creek he accused Shingas of tricking him. He then participated in the siege of Fort Pitt. He died in 1763, probably from small pox.

Slaughter, George (1739–1818)
Slaughter was major in the 12th Virginia Regiment and passed through Fort Pitt in April, 1780 while on his way to join George Rogers Clark in Kentucky. He later became lieutenant colonel of all Virginia forces in Kentucky. Slaughter served in the Virginia Assembly in 1784.

Smallman, Thomas
Smallman was a cousin and long-time associate of George Croghan. He was commissioned a lieutenant in the Pennsylvania Regiment on December 5, 1757. Smallman was serving as a captain at Fort Pitt in 1759. He was commissioned major on April 13, 1760 and was serving under Henry Bouquet at Presqu'Île. Smallman was taken prisoner by the Shawnee in 1763 and released in 1764. He accompanied Croghan on his mission to the Illinois in 1765 and was wounded in an attack at the mouth of the Wabash River. He then journeyed to Illinois in 1766. Smallman was serving as a justice of the peace in 1774.

Stanwix, John (circa 1690–1766)
Stanwix entered the army approximately 1706 and was commissioned a captain in 1739, Major in 1741, and lieutenant colonel in 1745. He became deputy quartermaster general in 1754. Stanwix was commissioned colonel of the 1st Battalion, 60th Regiment on January 1, 1756 and was placed in command in the southern district. He was

again placed in command in the south in 1759 and promoted to major general on June 19, 1759. Stanwix was relieved of command in 1760 and returned to England where he was promoted to lieutenant general on January 19, 1761. He later served as lieutenant governor of the Isle of Wight, colonel of the 8th Regiment, and a member of Parliament. He died at sea while crossing from Dublin in 1766.

Sullivan, Dennis
Sullivan was a trader active on the Pennsylvania frontier in the 1740s. He was an employee of Lazarus Lowry. Sullivan was present at Logstown during George Croghan council with the Ohio tribes in May, 1751.

Sumner, Jethro (circa 1733–1785)
Sumner served as a volunteer cadet in the Virginia Regiment in autumn, 1755 and was commissioned an ensign on July 12, 1756. He was serving on the frontier in Augusta County in 1757. Sumner served as a lieutenant in the 2nd Virginia Regiment in 1758. He was in the garrison at Fort Pitt during the summer of 1759. Sumner rose to the rank of brigadier general in the North Carolina troops in the American War of Independence.

Tamaqua (King Beaver) (d. circa 1770)
Tamaqua was a Delaware chief and the brother of Shingas. He was a leader of the faction that sought reconciliation with the British in 1758. He became chief of the Turkey Division of the Delaware on the death of Shingas in 1763. He participated in the Rebellion of 1763 but again led the peace faction after the rebellion.

Tanaghrisson (Half King) (d. 1754)
Tanaghrisson was a leader of the Ohio River Iroquois. He was principal spokesman at the conferences held at Logstown in May, 1751 and June, 1752. A friend of the British, he opposed the French incursion into the Ohio River Valley and demanded they withdraw. He accompanied George Washington on his mission to the French at Fort Rivière aux boeufs in December, 1753. He was at the forks of the

Ohio when Claude-Pierre Pécaudy de Contrecoeur took possession in April, 1754. Tanaghrisson was also present at the ambush of the party led by Joseph Coulon de Villiers de Jumonville on May 28, 1754. He died at Harris's Ferry on October 4, 1754.

Trent, William (1715–1787)

Trent was a merchant and trader from Lancaster, Pennsylvania. He had been commissioned a captain of a Pennsylvania company for the aborted expedition against Canada in 1746. He became active in the fur trade in Ohio in the late 1740s and reported on Native American activities against the French in 1747. Trent then searched the confluence of the Ohio River for a site to build a fort in 1753. He was commissioned a captain in the Virginia Regiment by Lieutenant Governor Robert Dinwiddie in January 1754. The next month, Trent constructed a storehouse at the mouth of Redstone Creek and left Edward Ward in command to build a fort at the forks of the Ohio. He later served in the Pennsylvania Regiment and participated Forbes' Expedition in 1758. Trent lost most of his holdings during the Rebellion of 1763 and spent three years in London in the 1770s representing himself and other "Suffering Traders" in an attempt to gain restitution from the government for their losses.

Van Braam, Jacob (1725–1784)

Van Braam was born in Bergen op Zoom, Holland and served as a lieutenant in the Dutch Army prior to immigrating to Fredericksburg, Virginia in 1752. He served as a French interpreter for George Washington on his mission to the French on the Ohio River in 1753. Van Braam was commissioned a lieutenant in Virginia Regiment on January 25, 1754. He fought at the Battle of the Great Meadows on July 3, 1754 and acted as interpreter during the capitulation negotiations. During the negotiations he translated the word *l'assasinat* as "killed" instead of assassinated. He was later accused of deliberately misinterpreting the terms of the capitulation. He served as a hostage in good faith for the terms of the surrender of Fort Necessity, which included the return of French hostages taken during the Jumonville skirmish. He was held prisoner in Canada until 1760. After his release Van Braam resigned his commission in the Virginia Regiment and took a captain's commission in the 60th Regiment. He retired on half-pay until the American War of Independence. He then served with the 60th Regiment in East Florida from 1775–1779 and was promoted to major in 1777. Van Braam retired in 1779 and is believed to have settled in France after the war.

Vickroy, Thomas (1754–1845)

Vickroy was a resident of Bedford County, Pennsylvania and served in the Bedford County militia during the American War of Independence. He served as an assistant to George Woods in 1784 and helped him to survey a portion of the city of Pittsburgh. He later became a postmaster in Bedford.

Waggener, Thomas (d. 1760)

Waggener served as an officer in the aborted expedition against Canada in 1746. He was commissioned a lieutenant in the Virginia Regiment, on February 2, 1754. He was wounded in the skirmish at Jumonville Glen on May 28, 1754 and fought at the Battle of Great Meadows, July 3, 1754. Waggener was promoted to captain on July 20, 1754 and commanded a company of Virginia rangers at the Battle of Monongahela on July 9, 1755. He then commanded Virginia forces on the South Branch of the Potomac from 1755–1758. He served on the Forbes Expedition in 1758 and in the garrison at Fort Pitt from December, 1758 until his death sometime in early 1760.

Ward, Edward

Ward, the half brother of George Croghan, was commissioned ensign in Williams Trent's company of the Virginia Regiment in January, 1754. He was in command at the forks of the Ohio River in April 1754 when he was forced to surrender the location to Claude-Pierre Pécaudy de Contrecoeur. Ward was commissioned a captain in the Pennsylvania Regiment on December 13, 1757 and served in the Forbes expedition of 1758. He was promoted to major on April 26, 1759. After the war he returned to the western trade. Ward occupied the grounds of Fort Pitt after it was abandoned in 1773.

Ward, Thomas
Ward was a trader who was present at Logstown during the council held there by George Croghan in May, 1751.

Washington, George (1732–1799)
Washington had begun his military career in 1752 as adjutant of Virginia militia for the Southern District with the rank of major. In 1753 he volunteered to deliver a message to the French on the Ohio River, ordering them to withdraw immediately. He was then commissioned lieutenant colonel of the Virginia Regiment on January 25, 1754, and was promoted to colonel in May 1754. He commanded the Virginia forces in the skirmish at Jumonville Glen on May 28, 1754, which triggered the French retaliation that resulted in his defeat at the Battle of Great Meadows on July 3, 1754. When the Virginia Regiment was disbanded in October, 1754 he resigned his commission rather than be demoted to captain of an independent company. Washington served as a volunteer aide-de-camp to General Braddock in 1755. He accepted a commission as colonel of the newly reorganized Virginia Regiment on August 31, 1755 and commanded the frontier defenses of Virginia until December 1758, when he resigned his commission after the capture of Fort Duquesne. He returned to the Ohio River Valley in 1770 to tour land granted to him and other veterans of the French and Indian War along the Kanawha River.

Wayne, Anthony (1745–1796)
Wayne was born in Chester County, Pennsylvania and became a land surveyor. He served as a representative for his county in the colonial assembly in 1774–1775 and was a member of the committee of safety in 1775. Wayne was commissioned colonel of the 4th Pennsylvania Regiment on January 3, 1776 and was placed in command at Fort Ticonderoga in June. He was promoted to brigadier general on February 21, 1777 and commanded divisions at the Battles of Brandywine and Germantown. He was given command of a light infantry corps in 1779 and captured Stony Point on July 16, 1779. After the surrender of Cornwallis, Wayne was sent south where he took possession of Charleston, South Carolina in December, 1782. Wayne retired

from the army after the war and returned to politics. It was not long before he returned to the army when was appointed him commander of the United State Army with the rank of major general on April 8, 1792. He decisively defeated the Ohio tribes at the Battle of Fallen Timbers on August 20, 1793 and negotiated the Treaty of Greenville on August 3, 1795. Wayne died of gout on December 15, 1796.

Weiser, Conrad (1696–1760)
Weiser was born in Württemberg in Germany and settled on the New York frontier with his family in 1709. He lived with the Mohawks in 1712–1713 and learned the Iroquois language. Weiser moved to the Tulpehocken Valley in Berks County, Pennsylvania in 1729. He soon began working for the Pennsylvania Government as an agent to the Iroquois. He served as colonel of the 1st Battalion, Pennsylvania Regiment during the French and Indian War. Weiser was the main architect of Pennsylvania Indian policy during the first half of the Eighteenth Century.

Williams, Joseph
Williams took out a warrant in 1792 for lands along Walnut Bottom Run on which the town of Beaver Falls, Pennsylvania now stands.

Wolf, The
The Wolf was the son of the Delaware chief, Ketiuscund. He escorted Frederick Christian Post during his mission to the Delaware villages in 1758. He also served as a scout and messenger for the British in 1759–1760.

Wood, Joseph (1712–1791)
Wood was born in Pennsylvania and moved to Georgia in 1774. He was severely wounded while serving in Canada in 1776. He later commanded the 2nd Pennsylvania Battalion and then the 3rd Pennsylvania Regiment. He resigned his commission and returned to Georgia in 1776. Wood served as a delegate from Georgia in the Continental Congress in 1777–1778.

Woods, George (d. 1796)

Woods was a surveyor and was living in the Juniata River Valley in 1753. He was taken prisoner at Bingham's Fort on June 11, 1755 but later released by his captors. Woods settled at Bedford, Pennsylvania and returned to surveying after the war. He became a leading citizen and represented Bedford County in the Pennsylvania Assembly in 1773. Woods was appointed colonel of the 2nd Battalion, Bedford County militia in 1776 and served as a member of the Supreme Executive Council of Pennsylvania in 1778–1779. He surveyed a portion of Pittsburgh in 1784.

Woods, John (1761–1816)

The son of Colonel George Woods, John was born in Bedford County, Pennsylvania and served in the Bedford County militia as a major. He was admitted to the bar in 1783. He assisted his father in hi survey of a portion of Pittsburgh in 1784. Woods was one of the first attorneys in Pittsburgh and soon became a leading citizen. He was commissioned a brigadier general in the militia on March 28, 1798. Woods was elected to the Pennsylvania Senate in 1797 and acted as speaker in 1800. He was elected to the House of Representatives in 1814 but never attended due to ill health.

Woodward, Henry

Woodward was a former naval officer who was commissioned a lieutenant in the Virginia Regiment on December 13, 1754. He served in Captain Thomas Waggener's company of Virginia rangers at the Battle of Monongahela. Woodward was promoted to captain on August 25, 1755 and served in the garrisons at Winchester, Fort Cumberland, and Vass's Fort from 1755–1758. He served on the Forbes Expedition in 1758. Woodward was stationed at Fort Ligonier in May, 1759. He was serving at Fort Chiswell on the southwest frontier in July, 1761. Woodward returned to England in late 1761 seeking an appointment to command a vessel on the Great Lakes.

Wright, John

John Wright was commissioned a lieutenant in a company from the lower counties (Delaware) on April 19, 1758. He was serving in the garrison at Fort Pitt in 1759 and was promoted to captain on May 24, 1759.

Ziegler, David (1748–1811)

Ziegler was a veteran of the American War of Independence and was commissioned to command a company from Pennsylvania in the First American Regiment. He was promoted to major in 1790. Ziegler was elected the first mayor of Cincinnati, Ohio in 1802 and became adjutant-general of Ohio in 1807.

Bibliography

The following is a select bibliography of the sources utilized in the editorial research for this edition:

Primary Sources:

Abbott, W. W., Dorothy Twohig, et. al., eds. *The Papers of George Washington: Colonial Series.* 10 Vols. Charlottesville, VA: University Press of Virginia, 1983–1995.

Butterfield, C. W., ed. *Journal of Capt. Jonathan Heart on the march with his company from Connecticut to Fort Pitt, in Pittsburgh, Pennsylvania, from the Seventh of September to the Twelfth of October, 1785, Inclusive: To Which Is Added the Dickinson-Harmar Correspondence of 1784–5.* Albany, NY: J. Munsell's Sons, 1885.

Grenier, Fernand, ed. *Papiers Contrecoeurs et autre documents concernant le conflit Anglo-Français sur l'Ohio de 1745 á 1756.* Quebec: Les presses universitaires Laval, 1952.

Kellogg, Louise Phelps, ed. *Frontier Advance on the Upper Ohio, 1778–1779.* Madison, WI: State Historical Society of Wisconsin, 1916.

Jordan, John W., ed. "The Journal of James Kenney." *Pennsylvania Magazine of History and Biography.* Vol. 37. Ed. By John W. Jordan.

Knox, John. *Historical Journal of the Campaigns in North-America for the Years 1757, 1758, 1759 and 1760.* London, 1769.

Linn, John B., and William H. Egle. *Pennsylvania Provincial Archives, Second Series.* Harrisburg, PA: B. F. Meyers, 1876.

Pennsylvania Provincial Council Minutes, Colonial Records. Harrisburg: Theo. Fenn & Co., 1851.

Wainwright, Nicholas D., ed. "George Croghan's Journal, 1759–1763." *The Pennsylvania Magazine of History and Biography.* Vol. 71, 1947.

Thwaites, Reuben Gold, ed. Early Western Journals, 1748–1765.

Secondary Sources:

Anderson, Niles. *The Battle of Bushy Run.* Harrisburg, PA: Pennsylvania Historical and Museum Commission, 1991

Bausman, Joseph. *History of Beaver County Pennsylvania and Its Centennial Celebration.* 2 volumes. New York: The Knickerbocker Press, 1904.

Brumwell, Stephen. *Redcoats: The British Soldier and War in the Americas 1755–1763.* New York: Cambridge University Press, 2001.

Cook, Ramsay, and Réal Bélanger, eds. *Dictionary of Canadian Biography.* 14 volumes, 1966–1998.

Gillett, Mary C. *The Army Medical Department, 1775–1818.* United States Army Historical Series. Washington DC: U.S. Government Printing Office, 1981.

Hanna, Charles A. *The Wilderness Trail, or the Ventures and Adventures of the Pennsylvania Traders on the Allegheny Path.* 2 Vols. New York: G. P. Putnam's Sons, 1911.

O'Meara, Walter. *Guns at the Forks.* Englewood Cliffs, NJ: Prentice-Hall, Inc., 1965.

Index

182

French bypass exploration of 21
French discovery of 22
Lake George
  French exploration of 21
Lake Huron 62
  French exploration of 21, 22
Lake Michigan
  French exploration of 21
Lake Ontario 62, 117
  French bypass exploration of 21
Lake Saint Clair
  French crossing of 22
Lake Superior
  French exploration of 21
Lamb, Caleb
  at Logstown 111
  identification 150
Lancaster County, Pennsylvania
  122
Laumet de Lamothe Cadillac, An-
  toine 62
Laurens, Henry
  identification 64, 150
Laurens, Henry, President
  illustration of 35
Lawrence County, Pennsylvania 58
Le Caron, Joseph 21, 62
  identification 151
Lee, Arthur
  and Fort McIntosh 37
  as Indian commissioner 50
  identification 65, 151
Lee, Thomas 65
Lee, William, Sergeant 66
  identification 151
  instructions to 48, 58
Leet, Daniel, Major 31
  identification 64, 151
  map of 120
  surveys Beaver, Pennsylvania 58
Legionville
  Wayne's camp at 56

Lehigh River 113
Le Marchand de Lignery, François-
  Marie, Captain 98
Lightfoot, Samuel
  council at Fort Pitt 82
  identification 98, 151
Ligonier, Sir John, Field Marshall
  90
  identification 151
Little Beaver Creek
  and boundary line 57
  Bouquet crosses 31
Lochry, Archibald, Colonel
  ambush of 46
  identification 65, 152
Logstown (Ambridge, Pennsylva-
  nia) 15, 105, 118
  abondonment of 115
  Bouquet at 29, 118
  Conrad Weiser visits 24
  council at 109, 111
  Dunkard at 111
  fate of 105
  foundation of 122
  George Croghan at 24
  Lee at 37
  location of 29, 116, 118,
    120
  locaton of 105, 106
  Post at 113, 115
  Washington at 24, 112
London, England 65, 118
  Stanwix sails for 84
Long Island 83
Loradakoin
  lead plate at 22
Louis XV, King 22
Lowry, Alexander
  dispatched to Cuyahoga 50
  identification 66, 152
Lowry, Lazarus 122
Loyalsock River 83

Vixan
  council at Fort Pitt 82

W

Wabash River
  Fort Vincennes on 55
  French control of 21
Waggener, Thomas, Captain
  council at Fort Pitt 82
  identification 97, 169
Wainwright's Island
  Washington on 24
Walnut Bottom Run
  Brodhead's lands on 60
Ward, Edward, Captain 63
  builds fort at forks of Ohio 76
  council at Fort Pitt 82
  identification 169
Ward, Thomas
  at Logstown 111
  identification 170
Washington, George, General
    33, 63
  accused of murder of Jumonville
    27
  and Mercer at Trenton 85
  appoints Gibson commander at
    Fort Pitt 45
  appoints Hand commander at Fort
    Pitt 32
  appoints McIntosh commander at
    Fort Pitt 32
  at Fort Necessity 76
  at Logstown 116, 118
  at the forks of the Ohio 75
  at Wills Creek 24
  crosses Allegheny on raft 24
  delivers message to French
    24, 76, 112
  identification 170
  illustration of 26
  letter to 39, 41, 45, 46

mission to French forts
    22, 24, 76
Washington County, Pennsylvania
    41
Waterford, Pennsylvania 62
Wayne, Anthony, General 69
  at Legionville 56
  Battle of Fallen Timbers 56
  identification 170
Weiser, Conrad 63, 109
  and the Wyandot 122
  identification of 106, 171
  location of Logstown 29, 116
  visits Logstown
    23, 106, 107, 109
Western University 15
Westmoreland County, Pennsylva-
    nia 28, 41, 46, 49, 91
  capture of Lyons 51
  Iroquois raids 42
Wheeling Creek
  killings at 39
Whig Party
  Agnew joins 15
Whiskey Rebellion (1794) 64
White Eyes, Delaware chief
    122
Whitehall, London, England
  William Pitt at 77, 86
Williams, Joseph 60
  identification 171
Wills Creek
  Washington at 24
Wolf, The
  escorts Post 116
  identification 123, 171
Womelsdorff, Pennsylvania 106
Wood, Joseph, Colonel 52
  identification 68, 171
Woods, George, Colonel
  identification 172
  surveys Pittsburgh 95

195

www.ingramcontent.com/pod-product-compliance
Lightning Source LLC
Chambersburg PA
CBHW060746100426

42813CB00032B/3418/J